AMERICA'S HANGAR
Steven F. Udvar-Hazy Center

SMITHSONIAN National Air and Space Museum

Editor, Dik Daso, Curator of Modern Military Aircraft

Third Edition   Washington, D.C.

I t is our distinct pleasure to welcome you to the Steven F. Udvar-Hazy Center, named for the Museum's main benefactor. With the opening of the Center, the Smithsonian Institution's National Air and Space Museum may now display the largest collection of aircraft and spacecraft from around the globe in a single location at Washington Dulles International Airport—it is America's Hangar.

Unveiled within this colossal structure are more than 300 aircraft and spacecraft displayed on three different viewing levels in two separate, immense hangars. Yet what you are experiencing remains a work in progress—the realization of a dream conceived decades ago to display the majority of our air and space treasures for all to enjoy.

The Boeing Aviation Hangar features craft from all eras of flight and from many countries. The Lockheed SR-71 on display is a world speed record holder and is still the fastest aircraft ever built. America's newest military aircraft, the Lockheed-Martin X-35B—the first aircraft in history to accomplish a short takeoff, supersonic run, and vertical landing on one mission—rests here. A spectacular collection of foreign and U.S.-built rockets and spacecraft from World War II through the present are featured in the James S. McDonnell Space Hangar, home to the Space Shuttle *Enterprise.* In the meantime, famous aircraft and spacecraft—like the *Winnie Mae,* Concorde, Boeing B-29 *Enola Gay,* and the Laser 200—can now be viewed as never before.

This new Center and the National Mall building are really one gigantic air and space museum separated only by distance. The visitor experience, however, is completely different in each. The Center's open hangar-like design allows us to display aircraft that could not even fit through the doors of the National Mall building. Looking skyward, the open ten-story structure allows us to display many of our collection in exciting realistic ways. It will be hard to forget the Curtiss P-40, hung as if attacking a convoy, or the inverted-gull-wing Vought Corsair, ready to "catch a wire" on an aircraft carrier. The aircraft that brought American passenger planes into the jet age, the Boeing 367-80, is on display. Though different, the combined museum experiences are complementary. The galleries in our original museum on the National Mall explore air and space flight throughout the ages in a more traditional, exhibitions-oriented way. America's Hangar is an awe-inspiring open showroom of amazing and rare air and space artifacts.

Think of this new museum as a centennial anniversary present and tribute to aviation and space exploration. It was just over a century ago that the Wright brothers flew for the first time. The first flight was only slightly shorter than the wingspan of the B-29 on display, but what a beginning! In this hangar you will find the history of aviation that was born on that windy December 1903 day on the sands of Kitty Hawk. Enjoy your visit!

J.R. Dailey
Director
National Air and Space Museum
Smithsonian Institution

Joseph T. Anderson
Deputy Director
Steven F. Udvar-Hazy Center
Smithsonian Institution

Contents

Planning, Design, and Construction of the Steven

IN JULY 1976, 30 YEARS AFTER CONGRESS authorized the establishment of the National Air Museum as part of the Smithsonian Institution, the National Air and Space Museum (NASM) opened the doors of its flagship museum on the Mall in Washington, D.C. Even as the Museum's staff was moving historic aircraft into this space, they realized that they would need a second facility to house the growing National Collection of aviation and space artifacts. The new building was large—three city blocks long—but the largest aircraft being relocated there was a Douglas DC-3, which started its flying career in 1936. How could the Museum tell the history of modern aviation and space-flight? Where could the Museum display the next generation of commercial airliners? How could the Museum ever bring the space shuttle *Enterprise,* which had just rolled off the assembly line, to downtown Washington?

F. Udvar-Hazy Center

by Lin Ezell

As early as the mid-1960s, proponents of a national air museum had been suggesting that the new Washington Dulles International Airport could meet the needs of the Smithsonian: it was within an hour's commute of the tourists who came to Washington; its runways were suitable for the arrival of large aircraft; and there was acreage available for long-term growth. But the Smithsonian and Congress first supported the construction of an aerospace museum in downtown Washington as part of the Institution's popular complex of museums. In this location, NASM has consistently attracted more visitors than any other museum in the world, routinely hosting more than 9 million visitors annually.

Before the Museum was built, the Smithsonian displayed aviation and space artifacts in a temporary building on the Mall and at the Arts and Industries Building, but the majority of its collection was stored, unseen, in Suitland, Maryland. Many of the aircraft had been at this cleared forested swamp in an area called Silver Hill, waiting for better quarters since the early 1950s. When the new Museum opened in 1976, however, many artifacts were left behind. And as the collections continued to grow, the 21-acre complex could not provide the quality of care museum artifacts deserve. NASM revived the idea of taking part of the collection to Dulles.

Throughout the 1980s, NASM made its case that a second facility at an active airfield was required to guarantee the future of its important collection. Dulles met all the Museum's requirements, including the support of airport and local authorities. In 1984, the Smithsonian submitted its first Congressional request for authorization to

OPPOSITE
The Udvar-Hazy Center is located on 176.5 acres in the southeast quadrant of Dulles International Airport, with easy access to a nearby runway and major highways.

ABOVE
Christine and Steven F. Udvar-Hazy on a tour of the construction site, April 2, 2002

Hensel Phelps Construction Co. built the huge aviation hangar in less than two years. ADF International, the structural steel subcontractor, partially fabricated the huge trusses at the factory and finished the job on-site.

Crane operators took each finished truss section to its designated location in the 984-foot-long hangar.

ADF bridged the trusses together in groups of four.

Using two cranes, the construction team raised the truss sections in place as a single unit.

Center truss sections were installed one by one.

ADF raised the first truss sections in late January 2002 and bolted together the final center section five months later.

Each of the 21 trusses in the vaulted hangar can accommodate the weight of two World War II fighter aircraft.

The Center's design reflects the airport environment.

build at Dulles. It took nearly a decade for lawmakers to pass legislation and provide funding. During those years, the collection had continued to grow, artifacts stored in substandard conditions had continued to degrade, and construction prices had soared. Encouraged by a guarantee of financial support from the Commonwealth of Virginia, Congress approved $8 million in 1993 to design the "Dulles Extension." Three years later in a second bill, Congress further authorized the Museum to proceed, but with the caveat that no federal money be spent on construction.

The Smithsonian had already begun to formally define its needs for the new facility. Hellmuth, Obata + Kassabaum (HOK), the architectural firm that had designed the Museum on the Mall, was again engaged to assist the Smithsonian. Working with collections experts, curators, and exhibit designers, HOK produced reports that quantified the facility in terms of size, structural and mechanical requirements, site and access needs, and environmental impact. By the time Congress approved design funds, airport officials had identified a 176.5-acre tract of land in Dulles' southeastern quadrant that was ideal for the Museum: less than a mile from a north-south runway, close to major highways, and with room for growth.

HOK and the Museum remained true to their original concept for a building that would meet the special needs of a large collection of aircraft and spacecraft—along with millions of visitors—but still fit the ambience of an airport. The design featured a large vaulted space, reminiscent of a dirigible hangar, for some 200 aircraft. The Museum told the designers that they wanted to hang many aircraft as if they were flying, and they needed to get the most display space for each construction dollar spent. The space shuttle *Enterprise,* along with some 135 other space vehicles, would be housed in the James S. McDonnell Space Hangar. Visitors would also be able to watch specialists restore aircraft, conduct research in the archives, take classes in an education center, and watch IMAX® movies. The total complex logged in at 760,000 square feet. While the Museum could have used even more space, officials understood the enormous fund-raising task ahead of them and approved a design that met their most immediate needs.

As part of a generous contribution from Virginia, the state funded all the site infrastructure needs of the project. In the spring of 2000, the Virginia Department of Transportation (VDOT) let a contract to clear land for the "Dulles Center." The land upon which the new facility would be built had been farmed since the Colonial period. When

ABOVE RIGHT
Another team of steelworkers built the frame for the IMAX® theater.

CURVED GLASS CURTAIN WALL OF LANDSIDE ELEMENT

The Donald D. Engen Tower is 164 feet high and gives visitors a "pilot's view" of the airport.

the airport bought the property in the 1950s, it planted the fields in pine trees, which were ready for harvesting when the contractors came onto the site. In the fall of 2000, the Smithsonian officially broke ground and honored the benefactor after whom the project was newly named: Steven F. Udvar-Hazy.

As the Smithsonian awarded the building contract to Hensel Phelps Construction Co. (HPCC) in the spring of 2001, VDOT sent in their second contractor team to complete utility installation, pave roads and the 2,000-car parking lot, and complete a link to Runway 1R-19L. Because the Institution was raising funds for construction while construction was ongoing, the Museum phased the project. HPCC would first build the huge aviation hangar and the architecturally stunning east wing, which would contain the theater, classrooms, food court, and other assets required by the 3 to 4 million visitors expected each year. The initial contract was let for $125,578,000. With an army of subcontractors, HPCC set two teams to work: one on the east wing and one on the hangar. Each worked north to south. Blessed by a dry, mild winter, construction crews flew through their schedule. The mighty hangar trusses, each of which could support the weight of up to two World War II fighters, were erected in less than six months. In April 2002, construction began on the space hangar. By the fall of 2002, the project under contract was more than three-quarters complete. Opening day, in December 2003, was timed to celebrate the anniversary of the Wright brothers' first flight on December 17, 1903.

ABOVE
The Donald D. Engen Observation Tower by moonlight

BELOW
VADM Don Engen, USN (Ret.) next to the model of a vision—the Udvar-Hazy Center

Admiral Donald D. Engen Observation Tower

DONALD D. ENGEN, the late Director of the National Air and Space Museum (1996–1999), was a tireless advocate of the need for the Udvar-Hazy Center. In 1984, he was instrumental in setting aside the land at Dulles International Airport while he was Administrator of the Federal Aviation Administration. Don continued his interest when he became NASM Director and contributed many ideas to the design of the new facility. He traveled the country to meet with aviation enthusiasts, telling them about the need for the Center and soliciting their support.

The Udvar-Hazy Center features an observation tower from which visitors can watch arriving and departing Washington Dulles International Airport air traffic. The tower has been named after Admiral Engen to honor his role in securing the

Piper J-3 Cub

First built in 1938, the Piper J-3 earned fame as a trainer and sport plane. Its success made the name "Cub" a generic term for light airplanes. The little yellow tail dragger remains one of the most recognized designs in aviation. J-3 Cubs and subsequent models are still found at fields around the world. Thousands of pilots who learned to fly in the Civilian Pilot Training Program trained in Cubs.

William T. Piper and Piper Aircraft are one of general aviation's greatest success stories. Piper took Gilbert Taylor's Tiger Kitten and E-2 designs and, with Walter Jamoneau, built the Taylor and Piper J-2, then the legendary Piper J-3. When production ended in 1947, 19,888 Piper Cubs had been built. This Cub was built in 1941 and accumulated more than 6,000 hours of flying time before being restored in 1975.

AIRCRAFT SPECIFICATIONS

Wingspan:	10.7 m (35 ft 3 in)
Length:	6.8 m (22 ft 5 in)
Height:	1.9 m (6 ft 8 in)
Weight, empty:	309 kg (680 lb)
Weight, gross:	554 kg (1,220 lb)
Top speed:	129 km/h (80 mph)
Engine:	Continental A-65, 65 hp
Manufacturer:	Piper Aircraft Corp., Lock Haven, Pa., 1941

TOP
The Piper Cub was the first aircraft to roost at the Udvar-Hazy Center. More than 300 air and spacecraft will follow.

BOTTOM
A Cub in action.

OPPOSITE
The National Air and Space Museum's Cub hung in the rafters of the Paul E. Garber Restoration Facility for many years until the Udvar-Hazy Center became a reality.

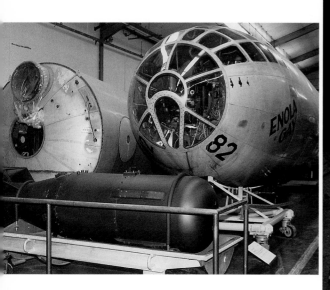

ABOVE AND RIGHT
The B-29 *Enola Gay* rested for many years in the Paul E. Garber Restoration Facility in Suitland, Maryland. Restoration took more than a decade.

BELOW
A rare look out the tail gunner's position in the B-29 *Enola Gay*— tight quarters, but an unmatched view.

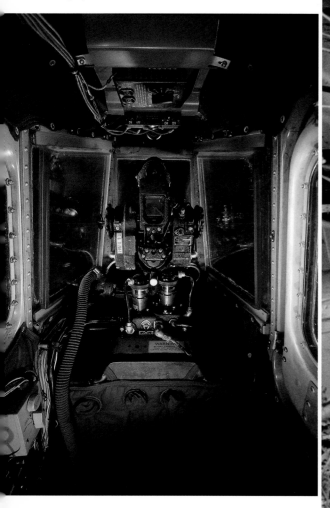

Boeing B-29 Superfortress
Enola Gay

Boeing's B-29 Superfortress was the most sophisticated propeller-driven bomber of World War II, and the first bomber to house its crew in pressurized compartments. Although designed to fight in the European theater, the B-29 found its niche on the other side of the globe. In the Pacific, B-29s delivered a variety of aerial weapons: conventional bombs, incendiary bombs, mines, and two nuclear weapons.

On August 6, 1945, this Martin-built B-29-45-MO dropped the first atomic weapon used in combat on Hiroshima, Japan. Three days later, *Bockscar* (on display at the U.S. Air Force Museum near Dayton, Ohio) dropped a second atomic bomb on Nagasaki, Japan. *Enola Gay* flew as the advance weather reconnaissance aircraft that day. A third B-29, *The Great Artiste,* flew as an observation aircraft on both missions.

AIRCRAFT SPECIFICATIONS

Wingspan:	43 m (141 ft 3 in)
Length:	30.2 m (99 ft)
Height:	9 m (27 ft 9 in)
Weight, empty:	32,580 kg (71,826 lb)
Weight, gross:	63,504 kg (140,000 lb)
Top speed:	546 km/h (339 mph)
Engines:	four Wright R-3350-57 Cyclone turbo-supercharged radials, 2,200 hp
Crew:	12 (Hiroshima mission)
Armament:	two .50 caliber machine guns
Ordnance:	"Little Boy" atomic bomb
Manufacturer:	Martin Co., Omaha, Nebr., 1945

In 1995, the *Enola Gay* became the center of an exhibition controversy at the National Air and Space Museum. The tail (top), forward fuselage and one propeller (center), and cockpit sections (seen here before restoration) were part of the display.

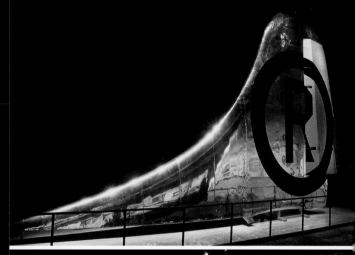

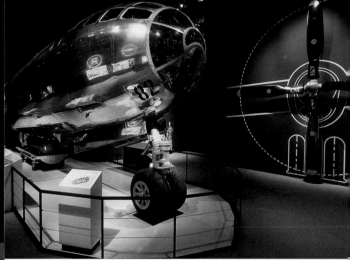

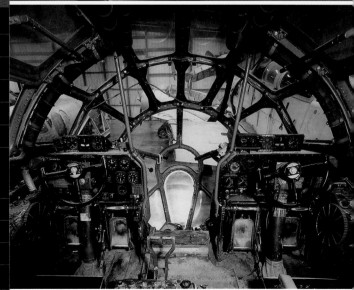

LEFT
Restoration specialist Scott Wood buffs the wing to a mirror-like finish.

BELOW
On a beautiful day in Washington, D.C., *Enola Gay* left her perch at the National Air and Space Museum in final preparation for the move to America's Hangar. Now, fully assembled, this historic aircraft is on display at the Udvar-Hazy Center.

TOP

The Boeing B-29 *Enola Gay* rests atop three massive electric lifts, elevated eight feet above the floor making room for other WW II vintage aircraft beneath her 140-foot wingspan.

BOTTOM

In the final stages of assembly, *Enola Gay* is back together for the first time in more than 40 years.

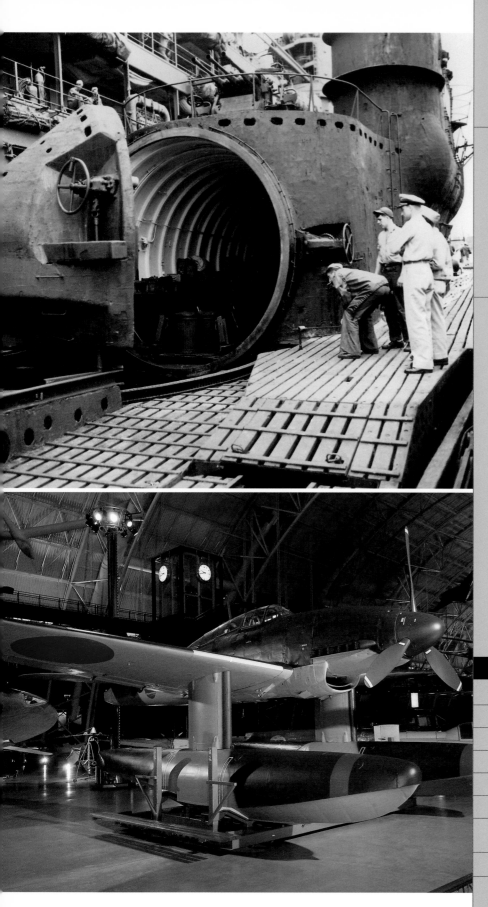

Aichi M6A1 Seiran

Aichi chief engineer Toshio Ozaki designed the Seiran (Clear Sky Storm) during World War II to fulfill a requirement for a bomber that could operate exclusively from a submarine. Japanese war planners devised the idea as a means for striking directly at the United States mainland and other distant strategic targets, such as the Panama Canal. To support Seiran operations, the Japanese developed a special fleet of submarine aircraft carriers to bring the Seirans within striking distance.

No Seiran ever saw combat, but the Seiran-submarine weapons system represents an ingenious blend of aviation and marine technology. This M6A1 was the last airframe built and is the only surviving Seiran in the world. Allied forces discovered it on the Japanese mainland after the war.

AIRCRAFT SPECIFICATIONS

Wingspan:	12.3 m (40 ft 3 in)
Length:	11.6 m (38 ft 2 in)
Height:	4.6 m (15 ft)
Weight, empty:	3,310 kg (7,282 lb)
Weight, gross:	4,445 kg (9,800 lb)
Top speed:	475 km/h (295 mph)
Engine:	Aichi AE1P Atsuta 32, 12-cylinder, liquid-cooled, inverted V, 1,400 hp
Crew:	2
Armament:	flexible rear-firing 13 mm Type-2 machine gun
Ordnance:	one 800–850-kg or two 250-kg bombs
Manufacturer:	Aichi Kokuki K. K., Eitoku, Japan, 1945

OPPOSITE TOP
Seiran's wings folded so that it fit inside a submarine.

OPPOSITE BOTTOM
The world's only remaining Aichi Seiran was captured
by Allied forces after WW II.

ABOVE
Restoration specialists apply the finishing touches to
the Seiran.

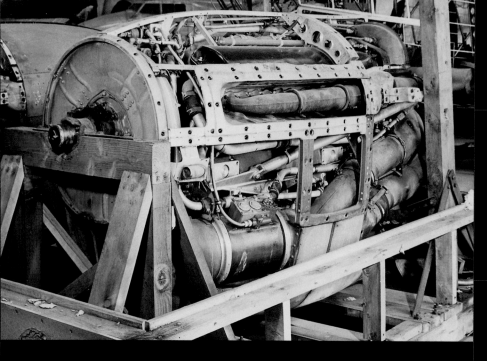

ABOVE
The powerful Allison engine was liquid cooled and a pair could deliver more than 2,800 horsepower.

BELOW
Here, the P-38 nose awaits restoration at the Paul E. Garber Restoration Facility.

Lockheed P-38 Lightning

From 1942 to 1945, U.S. Army Air Forces pilots flew the P-38 over Europe, the Mediterranean, and the Pacific; from the frozen Aleutian Islands to the sun-baked deserts of North Africa. Lockheed engineer Clarence "Kelly" Johnson and a team of designers created one of the most successful twin-engine fighters ever flown by any nation. In the Pacific Theater, Lightning pilots downed more Japanese aircraft than pilots flying any other AAF warplane.

On April 16, 1945, while at Wright Field, Ohio, for tests, Major Richard I. Bong, America's leading fighter ace, flew this aircraft. Bong had planned to fly for an hour to evaluate an experimental method of interconnecting the movement of the throttle and propeller control levers. His flight ended prematurely when his right engine exploded before he could conduct the experiment.

AIRCRAFT SPECIFICATIONS

Wingspan:	15.8 m (52 ft 0 in)
Length:	11.7 m (37 ft 10 in)
Height:	2.9 m (9 ft 10 in)
Weight, empty:	6,345 kg (14,100 lb)
Weight, gross:	7,965 kg (17,699 lb)
Engines:	two Allison V-1710-89/91, liquid-cooled in-line, 1,425 hp
Crew:	1
Armament:	one 20 mm Hispano AN-M2C cannon. Four .50 caliber Browning machine guns. External bomb load of 4,000 lbs or ten 5-inch rockets
Manufacturer:	Lockheed Aircraft Corp., Burbank, Calif., November 6, 1943

The P-38 Lightning saw combat in every theater of operations during World War II—from Europe to the Pacific.

The Lightning has been restored to accurately represent its World War II appearance during testing at Wright Field.

Bell No. 2
Rocket Belt

Often called the Jet Pack, Jet Flying Belt, Jet Belt, or Jet Vest, the rocket belt is a small personal-propulsion device. Strapped on the back, it enables a person to fly short distances using low rocket power produced by a noncombusting gas.

The rocket belt concept appeared in Buck Rogers comic strips as early as 1929. Wendell Moore of Bell Aerosystems Company was the first to develop a working version in the mid-1950s. In the 1960s, the U.S. military seriously considered equipping combat soldiers with the device, but its duration of just a few seconds was too limited. A jet-powered version with longer duration was later developed, but it too proved inadequate. Today Jet Packs are used mainly in expositions, in movie stunts, in football game half-time shows, and at other events.

A pilot tests a Bell Company Rocket Belt, ascending more than a hundred feet in seconds.

Ruhrstahl X-4 Missile

The German X-4 was a small air-to-air missile of World War II that could be fired at heavily armed Allied bombers from a distance. To prevent jamming, guidance was by wires running between the missile and its launch aircraft rather than by radio. Slated for use on the Me 262 jet fighter, the X-4 could also have been fired from such piston-engine aircraft as the Ju 88, Ju 388, and Fw 190, all of which launched test missiles beginning in August 1944.

A BMW 109-548 liquid-fuel rocket engine powered the missile. Ruhrstahl produced 1,000 X-4 airframes in late 1944, but an Allied air raid destroyed the BMW engines and production lines, a blow from which the program never recovered. The Smithsonian obtained this missile from the U.S. Navy in 1948.

VEHICLE SPECIFICATIONS

Length:	2 m (6 ft 6.8 in)
Weight:	60 kg (132 lb)
Weight, warhead:	20 kg (44 lb)
Range:	5.5 km (3 mi)
Thrust:	294–1,370 N (66–309 lb)
Propellants:	Tonka 250, SV-Stoff
Manufacturer:	Ruhrstahl

Rheintochter R I Missile

The Rheintochter (Rhine Maiden) R I was an experimental German two-stage antiaircraft missile tested in the last year of World War II. Built by the Rheinmetall-Borsig company for the Luftwaffe, it was one of the largest solid-fuel rockets of the war. The R I was to be supplanted by the R III, a liquid-fuel missile with two side-mounted solid-fuel boosters that enabled it to reach a higher altitude. However, only six R IIIs were ever launched, as opposed to 82 R I missiles.

The Smithsonian acquired this Rheintochter R I from the U.S. Navy in 1969. It was displayed in the National Air and Space Museum from 1976 to the early 1980s. In 2002 it was restored to its original condition and paint scheme for exhibit at the Steven F. Udvar-Hazy Center.

VEHICLE SPECIFICATIONS

Length:	5.6 m (18 ft)
Weight:	1,100 kg (2,425 lb)
Weight, warhead:	150 kg (332 lb)
Range:	12.1 km (7.5 mi)
Thrust:	734,000 N (165,000 lb) booster, 39,144 N (8,800 lb) sustainer
Propellant:	solid diglycol rocket motor
Manufacturer:	Rheinmetall-Borsig, Germany

Hs 293 A-1 Missile

Germany developed the Hs 293 air-launched missile in World War II for use against ships or ground targets. It was basically a glide bomb assisted by a liquid-fuel rocket that fired for 10 seconds. The Hs 293 was carried under the wings or in the bomb bay of an He 111, He 177, Fw 200, or Do 217 aircraft. Its warhead was a modified SC 500 bomb containing Trialene 105 high explosive. A bombardier guided the missile by means of a joystick and radio control.

Beginning in mid-1943, Hs 293s sank several Allied ships, mostly in the Mediterranean Theater. Although Germany developed many experimental versions, only the Hs 293 A-1 was produced in quantity.

VEHICLE SPECIFICATIONS

Length:	3.6 m (11 ft 9 in)
Weight, loaded:	1,045 kg (2,304 lb)
Weight, warhead:	295 g (649 lb)
Range:	18 km (11 mi)
Thrust:	5,870 N (1,320 lb)
Propellants:	hydrogen peroxide, sodium permanganate
Manufacturer:	Henschel Flugzeugwerke

Loon Missile

Also called the JB-2 by the U.S. Army Air Forces, the Loon was an American copy of the German pulsejet-powered V-1 "buzz bomb" of World War II. The long tube at the rear is the air-breathing pulsejet engine.

Developed late in the war, the Loon was first test launched in October 1944. Loons could be launched from the ground, ships, or aircraft, but they were never used in combat. However, U.S. Navy and Army Air Forces personnel working with Loons gained invaluable experience in handling missiles. The program was canceled in 1950. The faster and more powerful Regulus missile replaced the Loon.

VEHICLE SPECIFICATIONS

Length:	8.2 m (27 ft)
Weight, loaded:	2,700 kg (6,000 lb)
Weight, warhead:	998 kg (2,200 lb)
Range:	242 km (150 mi)
Thrust:	2,224 N (500 lb)
Propellant:	gasoline
Manufacturer:	Ford Motor Co.

TM-61C Matador Cruise Missile

The TM-61C was the second version of the surface-to-surface U.S. Air Force Matador cruise missile. It carried a nuclear warhead and flew at subsonic speeds at an altitude of up to 13 kilometers (8 miles). The TM-61C was boosted during its launch by a solid-fuel rocket engine (not displayed here), which fired for less than three seconds and then was jettisoned. A jet engine then powered it the rest of the way to the target. Ground-based microwave emitters assisted the missile in finding its target. However, these limited the missile's range to that of line-of-sight transmissions and could be jammed.

The TM-61C was deployed at various sites in Europe and Asia from 1957 to 1962 and was replaced by the more advanced Mace cruise missile.

VEHICLE SPECIFICATIONS

Length:	12 m (39 ft 6 in)
Wingspan:	8.7 m (28 ft 7 in)
Weight:	5,400 kg (12,000 lb)
Speed:	1,040 km/h (650 mph)
Thrust, booster:	235,754 N (53,000 lb)
Thrust, sustainer:	16,458 N (3,700 lb)
Range:	1,000 km (620 mi)
Manufacturer:	Martin Co.

SA-2 Guideline Missile

Developed and made in the Soviet Union, the SA-2 has been used more widely than any other air defense missile in the world. In the Soviet Union it was called the Dvina; in the West it was known by its NATO code name, SA-2 Guideline (SA meaning surface-to-air). The SA-2 became operational in 1959 and was acquired by all Soviet client states. In 1960 an SA-2 downed the American U-2 spy plane piloted by Francis Gary Powers.

The SA-2 had a solid-fuel booster and a liquid-fuel second stage. Many countries made their own versions of the missile. This one, meant for export, is mounted on a transporter and required a separate launcher. SA-2s are still in use today.

VEHICLE SPECIFICATIONS

Length:	10.5 m (34 ft 6 in)
Weight, warhead:	129 kg (287 lb)
Range:	50 km (31 mi)
Propellants:	solid fuel, booster; liquid fuel, sustainer
Manufacturer:	Volkhov Defense Systems, U.S.S.R.

Balloonamania

by Tom Crouch and Suzanne Lewis

THE BROTHERS JOSEPH AND ETIENNE Montgolfier sent their first balloon aloft from the town square of Annonay, France, on June 4, 1783. It was a simple paper and fabric bag, 11 meters (35 feet) in diameter, filled with hot air. The event marked the beginning of a decade of great hot air and gas balloon flights in Europe and America.

The knowledge that human beings had actually taken to the sky after centuries of dreaming generated great popular excitement. "The novelty of the thing is so great," an American visitor to Paris remarked, "that it engrosses half the talk and attention of the city." Benjamin Franklin agreed. "All the conversation here at present turns upon the Balloons," he said to a friend, "and the means of managing them so as to give Men the Advantage of Flying."

The Balloon and Popular Culture
The balloon had an immediate impact on popular culture. Beverages and dances commemorated this wonder of the age. Clothing and hat styles were inspired by the colorful craft rising above the rooftops of Paris and London.

Balloon motifs decorated items of furniture, jewelry, ceramics, boxes, wallpaper, fans, upholstery fabric, and dozens of other items. The objects in this display case, dating from 1783 through the twentieth century, illustrate the continuing popularity of decorative themes involving balloons and airships.

TOP TO BOTTOM
Angoulême porcelain cup
Shagreen diptych case
French fan leaf
Jewel coffret with balloon decoration

RIGHT
Acajou Louis XVI poudreuse

OPPOSITE
Acajou Louis XVI secrétaire abattant

ABOVE
Angoulême porcelain saucer and cup

LEFT
Walnut chair

A Chronology of Selected Balloon Flights, 1783–1793

1783

June 4: Joseph and Etienne Montgolfier, sons of a paper manufacturer from Annonay, France, fly a small balloon in public for the first time.

Aug. 27: J. A. C. Charles flies the first small hydrogen-filled balloon from the Champ de Mars, a cavalry parade ground in the heart of Paris.

Sept. 19: The Montgolfier brothers send the first living creatures aloft from the palace at Versailles, outside Paris. The sheep, rooster, and duck return safely to earth a few minutes later.

Nov. 21: Pilâtre de Rozier and the Marquis d'Arlandes become the first human beings to make a free flight aboard a Montgolfier hot air balloon.

Nov. 25: Francesco Zambecarri, an Italian living in London, launches the first small unmanned balloon in England.

Dec. 1: J. A. C. Charles and M. N. Robert make the first flight aboard a hydrogen-filled balloon.

1784

Feb. 25: Italian aeronaut Paolo Andreani makes the first balloon flight outside of France.

June 24: Peter Carnes, a lawyer and tavern keeper from Bladensburg, Maryland, sends the first American aloft on a tethered balloon flight, a 13-year-old Baltimore lad named Edward Warren.

Sept. 15: Vincenzo Lunardi, secretary to the Neapolitan ambassador, makes the first free flight from London.

1785

Jan. 7: J. P. F. Blanchard, a French aeronaut, and Dr. John Jeffries, an American loyalist living in England, make the first flight across the English Channel.

1793

Jan. 9: J. P. F. Blanchard makes the first free flight from American soil, traveling from Philadelphia to Deptford Township, New Jersey.

ABOVE
Louis XVI commode

BELOW
Gold-tooled red leather scent bottle case

RIGHT
Louis XVI carved gift gesso and wood wall mirror

Boeing 367-80 "Dash 80"

U.S. civil aviation entered the jet age on July 15, 1954, when the Boeing 367-80, or "Dash 80," first took flight. Designed for the U.S. Air Force as a jet tanker-transport, this airplane was the prototype for America's first commercial jet airliner, the Boeing 707.

Boeing began designing the "Dash 80" without a contract in 1952. In 1954 the Air Force purchased the first of 820 KC-135 tankers, as the modified version was designated. At Pan American's request, Boeing widened the fuselage to accommodate six-across seating for airline use. This larger aircraft became the Boeing 707, of which 855 were built between 1957 and 1992. The "Dash 80" tested many new technologies, including new engines and engine nacelles, different wing shapes, and a variety of flaps and control surfaces, before it was donated to the Smithsonian in 1972. Boeing restored it in 1995.

TOP TO BOTTOM
The "Dash 80" was towed from Dulles International Airport to the Udvar-Hazy Center earlier than planned to avoid Hurricane Isabel's arrival in the DC area. The aircraft is seen here in position at the Hazy Center.

The beautiful Boeing "Dash 80" in flight

AIRCRAFT SPECIFICATIONS

Wingspan:	39.4 m (129 ft 8 in)
Length:	39 m (127 ft 10 in)
Height:	11.6 m (38 ft)
Weight, empty:	41,786 kg (92,120 lb)
Weight, gross:	86,184 kg (190,000 lb)
Top speed:	937 km/h (582 mph)
Engines:	four Pratt and Whitney JT3D, 7,711 kg (17,000 lb) thrust
Manufacturer:	Boeing Aircraft Co., Seattle, Wash., 1954

Boeing 307 Stratoliner
Clipper Flying Cloud

First flown in late 1938, the Boeing 307 was the first airliner with a pressurized fuselage. It could carry 33 passengers in great comfort and cruise at 6,096 meters (20,000 feet), while maintaining a cabin pressure of 2,438 meters (8,000 feet). This enabled the Stratoliner to fly above most bad weather, thereby providing a faster and smoother ride.

The Stratoliner incorporated the wings, tail, and engines of the Boeing B-17C bomber. The wide fuselage was fitted with sleeper berths and reclining seats. Ten Stratoliners were built. The prototype was lost in an accident, but five were delivered to TWA and three were purchased by Pan American Airways. TWA owner Howard Hughes purchased a heavily modified version for his personal use. The airplane displayed here was flown by Pan American as the *Clipper Flying Cloud*. Boeing restored it in 2001.

AIRCRAFT SPECIFICATIONS

Wingspan:	32.7 m (107 ft 3 in)
Length:	22.7 m (74 ft 4 in)
Height:	6.3 m (20 ft 9 in)
Weight, empty:	13,749 kg (30,310 lb)
Weight, gross:	19,051 kg (42,000 lb)
Top speed:	396 km/h (246 mph)
Engines:	four Wright GR-1820 Cyclones, 900 hp
Manufacturer:	Boeing Aircraft Co., Seattle, Wash., 1940

TOP TO BOTTOM

The sleek silver appearance marked the Stratoliner as a luxurious transport. Interior ammenities were much more comfortable than most commercial airliners today.

The Stratoliner made it to the Hazy Center on time despite an unfortunate crash landing in Elliott Bay, just west of downtown Seattle, WA, on March 28, 2002. The Boeing restoration team repaired and restored the plane and flew it to Dulles International Airport in 2003.

Concorde

The first supersonic airliner to enter service, the Concorde flew thousands of passengers across the Atlantic at twice the speed of sound for over 25 years. Designed and built by Aérospatiale of France and the British Aircraft Corporation, the graceful Concorde was a stunning technological achievement that could not overcome serious economic problems.

In 1976, Air France and British Airways jointly inaugurated Concorde service to destinations around the globe. Carrying up to 100 passengers in great comfort, the Concorde catered to first-class passengers for whom speed was critical. It could cross the Atlantic in fewer than four hours—half the time of a conventional jet airliner. However, its high operating costs resulted in very high fares that limited the number of passengers who could afford to fly it. These problems and a shrinking market eventually forced the reduction of service until all Concordes were retired in 2003.

In 1989, Air France signed a letter of agreement to donate a Concorde to the National Air and Space Museum upon the aircraft's retirement. On June 12, 2003, Air France honored that agreement, donating Concorde F-BVFA to the Museum upon the completion of its last flight. This aircraft was the first Air France Concorde to open service to Rio de Janeiro, Washington, D.C., and New York and (upon retirement) had flown 17,824 hours.

AIRCRAFT SPECIFICATIONS

Wingspan:	25.56 m (83 ft 10 in)
Length:	61.66 m (202 ft 3 in)
Height:	11.3 m (37 ft 1 in)
Weight, empty:	79,265 kg (174,750 lb)
Weight, gross:	181,435 kg (400,000 lb)
Top speed:	2,179 km/h (1,350 mph)
Engines:	Four Rolls-Royce/SNECMA Olympus 593 Mk 602, 17,259 kg (38,050 lb) thrust each
Manufacturer:	Société Nationale Industrielle Aérospatiale, Paris, France, and British Aircraft Corporation, London, United Kingdom

The majestic Concorde touches down for the final time at Dulles International Airport. The towering tail will be easy to locate from any location on the Udvar-Hazy Center floor.

Lear Jet Model 23

The first Lear Jets, the Model 23 Continentals, were the first products of the original Lear Jet Corporation for the new field of business and personal jet aviation. So significant was the design that for years "Lear Jet" was synonymous with "bizjet." William P. Lear Sr. initiated the Lear Jet's development in 1959. The aircraft drew upon the structural quality of the Swiss AFA P-16 strike-fighter and featured a fuselage that narrowed at each side where the wing and engine nacelles extended outward—a design concept known as "area rule"—to provide smooth airflow around the engines.

Successive Lear Jet models set many speed records. The Lear Jet line is now part of the Bombardier Aerospace family, which includes Challenger and Global Express aircraft. This is the second Lear Jet built and the first production Model 23. Lear Jet used it as a test aircraft.

AIRCRAFT SPECIFICATIONS

Wingspan:	10.8 m (35 ft 7 in)
Length:	13.2 m (43 ft 3 in)
Height:	3.8 m (12 ft 7 in)
Weight, empty:	2,790 kg (6,150 lb)
Weight, gross:	5,783 kg (12,750 lb)
Top speed:	903 km/h (561 mph)
Engines:	two General Electric CJ 610-1 turbojets, 1,293 kg (2,850 lb) thrust
Manufacturer:	Lear Jet Corp., Wichita, Kans., 1964

TOP TO BOTTOM

Lear Jets easily cruised above the clouds and most airliners, providing a smooth and speedy flight.

The Model 23 is tucked carefully between the tails of the Boeing "Dash 80" and the French Concorde on the floor at the Udvar-Hazy Center.

Dassault Falcon 20

Wendy, FedEx's first aircraft, started the overnight air express industy on April 17, 1973.

Flying this Dassault Falcon 20, Federal Express revolutionized the air express industry in 1973 when it pioneered the overnight delivery of high-priority packages. FedEx purchased 33 of the popular French Dassault Falcon 20 business jets as its first aircraft, modifying each with a cargo door and a strengthened floor. The Falcon was fast and reliable, had an excellent payload for its size, and could reach any point in the United States from the company's Memphis, Tennessee, hub. This airplane, Federal Express's first, was named *Wendy,* after the daughter of FedEx founder Frederick W. Smith. FedEx donated it to the Smithsonian in 1983.

Derived from the Mystère IV fighter, the Falcon was originally designed to carry 10 passengers. Almost 500 airplanes were produced from 1963 through 1983.

AIRCRAFT SPECIFICATIONS

Wingspan:	16.3 m (53 ft 6 in)
Length:	17.2 m (56 ft 4 in)
Height:	5.7 m (17 ft 7 in)
Weight, empty:	7,230 kg (15,940 lb)
Weight, gross:	13,000 kg (28,660 lb)
Top speed:	862 km/h (535 mph)
Engines:	two General Electric CF700-2D turbofans, 1,983 kg (4,315 lb) thrust
Manufacturer:	Avions Marcel Dassault/Breguet Aviation, Paris, France, 1973

Pitts Special S-1C
Little Stinker

The oldest surviving Pitts Special, *Little Stinker* was the second aircraft constructed by Curtis Pitts. Pitts introduced the S-1 in 1945, the first of a famous line that dominated aerobatic competition throughout the 1960s and 1970s because of their small size, light weight, short wingspan, and extreme agility. Subsequent models still fly in all aerobatic categories and are standard aircraft for advanced aerobatic training.

Betty Skelton bought this airplane in 1948, and with it she won the 1949 and 1950 International Feminine Aerobatic Championships. Her impressive flying skill and public relations ability heightened awareness of both aerobatics and the Pitts design. Skelton sold *Little Stinker* in 1951, but she and her husband later reacquired it and donated it to the Smithsonian. A volunteer crew restored it from 1996 to 2001.

TOP TO BOTTOM

Betty Skelton had this brilliant red and white sunburst scheme painted onto the Pitts S-1C after she won her second Feminine Aerobatic Champion title. Now *Little Stinker* welcomes visitors to the Udvar-Hazy Center suspended upside down in the second level entryway.

A passing pilot snapped this photograph of Skelton while she was flying over Florida.

This dedicated volunteer crew restored *Little Stinker* over a six-year period at the Paul E. Garber Restoration Facility. Left to right: George Rousseau, Roger Guest, Joe Fichera, and Cindy Rousseau.

The *Little Stinker,* resplendent in its new fabric and paint, sparkles in the sun at its rollout. Pitts Specials are still popular aerobatic and training aircraft.

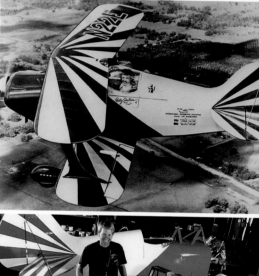

AIRCRAFT SPECIFICATIONS

Wingspan:	4.9 m (16 ft 10 in)
Length:	4.4 m (14 ft 6 in)
Height:	1.7 m (5 ft 6 in)
Weight:	257 kg (568 lb)
Top speed:	257 km/h (160 mph)
Engine:	Continental C85-8FJ, 85 hp
Builder:	Curtis Pitts, 1946

Loudenslager
Laser 200

With the Laser 200, Leo Loudenslager won an unprecedented seven U.S. National Aerobatic Champion titles between 1975 and 1982, as well as the 1980 World Champion title. The airplane originated as a Stephens Akro, a sleek aerobatic design, but by 1975 Loudenslager had completely modified the airplane with a new forward fuselage, wings, tail, and cockpit. The Laser 200 proved lighter, stronger, and more powerful, enabling Loudenslager to perform sharper and more difficult maneuvers.

Loudenslager's legacy is evident in the tumbling and twisting but precise routines flown by current champions and air show pilots. The Laser 200 heavily influenced the look and performance of the next generation of aerobatic aircraft, including the Extra, which dominated competition throughout the 1990s.

ABOVE
The Laser 200 was the first aircraft to be suspended at the Udvar-Hazy Center. Dorothy Cochrane, aircraft curator, admires the display.

BELOW
Leo Loudenslager's helmet and flightsuit are displayed in the Aerobatic Case along with flight clothing from famed aerobatic pilots Bob Hoover, Patty Wagstaff, and Suzanne Oliver.

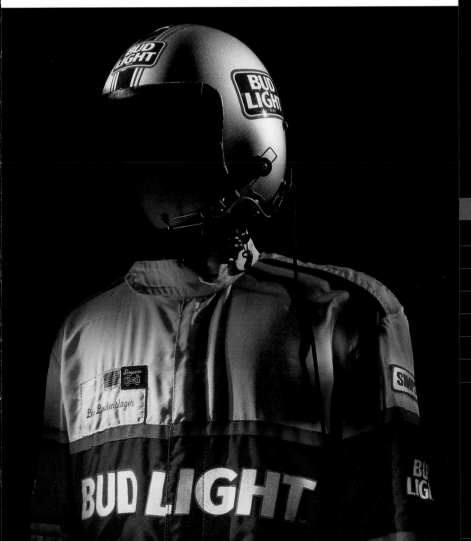

AIRCRAFT SPECIFICATIONS

Wingspan:	8 m (26 ft 2 in)
Length:	5.5 m (18 ft 8 in)
Height:	1.6 m (5 ft 5 in)
Weight:	400 kg (885 lb)
Top speed:	370 km/h (230 mph)
Engine:	Lycoming IO-360-A1A, 200 hp
Builder:	Leo Loudenslager, 1971

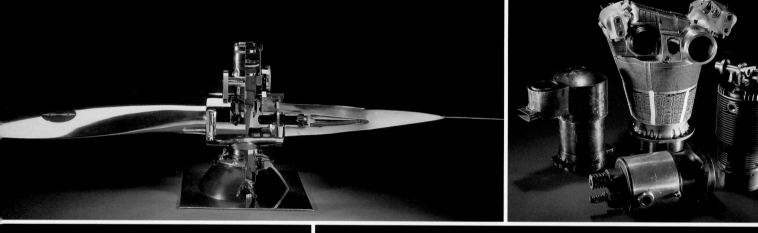

Aircraft Propulsion

ON THE MORNING of December 17, 1903, the first aeronautical propulsion system—a gas engine, propellers, and the equipment needed to make them operate—took to the air in the Wright *Flyer*. The aeronautical community continued to refine that system for heavier-than-air flight until the introduction of the gas turbine engine in the 1940s revolutionized the design and use of aircraft.

The objects displayed here at Udvar-Hazy include reciprocating internal combustion and gas turbine engines as well as the components and support technologies that make up aeronautical propulsion systems. These artifacts reveal the multiple approaches to improving the performance of aeronautical propulsion technology during the twentieth century.

OPPOSITE TOP LEFT
Taft-Peirce V-8 engine, 1911

OPPOSITE TOP RIGHT
General Electric Type C-series Turbosupercharger Cutaway, World War II

OPPOSITE CENTER LEFT
Hamilton Standard Controllable-Pitch Propeller Cutaway, 1933

OPPOSITE CENTER RIGHT
Engine cylinders, 1903–1950

OPPOSITE BOTTOM LEFT
Naval Air Technical Arsenal, Kugisho Ne-20 Turbojet, Japan, World War II

OPPOSITE BOTTOM RIGHT
Lycoming XR-7755-3 Radial 36, 1945

RIGHT TOP TO BOTTOM
Manufacturer's employee badges, 1920–1945

Pratt & Whitney R-1340 Wasp tools and toolbox, 1927

Rockets & Engines

Jupiter S-3 Rocket Engine

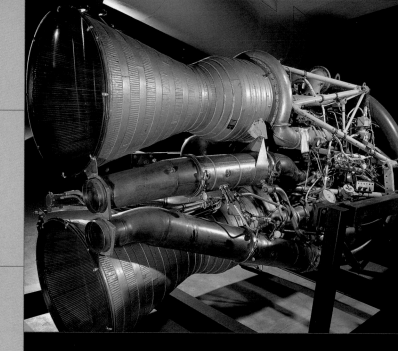

A modification of the Redstone engine, the S-3 powered the Jupiter missile, the first U.S. intermediate-range ballistic missile. Rocketdyne began developing the Jupiter engine in 1956. The Jupiter missile was activated in 1958 and was used until 1963. A modified version with additional upper stages, called the Juno II, was developed to launch spacecraft. Junos launched two Pioneer unmanned lunar probes in the late 1950s and put the Explorer 7, 8, and 11 satellites into Earth orbit.

VEHICLE SPECIFICATIONS

Length:	3.6 m (11 ft 10 in)
Thrust:	667,000 N (150,000 lb)
Propellants:	liquid oxygen, RP-1 (kerosene)
Manufacturer:	Rocketdyne Div., North American Aviation

Navaho Rocket Engine

This two-chambered, liquid-fuel rocket engine served as the booster for the Navaho missile, which was powered by two ramjets. The huge, vertically launched intercontinental cruise missile was designed to strike a target up to 8,850 kilometers (5,500 miles) away. However, the Navaho never became operational. Its unsuccessful testing program and enormous development cost, which had reached almost a billion dollars, caused the program to be cancelled in 1957.

The Navaho was an important stage in the evolution of American large-scale liquid-fuel engines, including those for the Redstone, Jupiter, Thor, and Atlas missiles, Saturn V Apollo launch vehicle, and the Space Shuttle.

VEHICLE SPECIFICATIONS

Length:	2.7 m (8 ft 9 in)
Thrust:	1,070,000 N (240,000 lb)
Propellants:	liquid oxygen, kerosene
Manufacturer:	North American Aviation

Redstone Missile

The first U.S. large-scale, liquid-fuel missile to become operational, the Redstone was one of the most historically important developments in U.S. rocket technology. The Jupiter-C, a Redstone modified with greater thrust and upper stages, placed Explorer 1, the first U.S. artificial satellite, into orbit in 1958. In 1961 a further modified Mercury-Redstone rocket launched the first American into space, Alan B. Shepard Jr.

The Redstone made its first successful flight in 1953 and became operational in 1958. As a missile, it had a range of 320–400 kilometers (200–250 miles) and could carry a conventional or nuclear warhead. The all-solid-fuel Pershing missile replaced the Redstone in 1964. The rocket displayed here is a partial cutaway.

VEHICLE SPECIFICATIONS

Length:	21 m (69 ft)
Weight, loaded:	20,412 kg (45,000 lb)
Thrust:	333,617 N (75,000 lb)
Propellants:	liquid oxygen and alcohol
Manufacturer:	Chrysler Corp., Missile Div.

V-2 Combustion Chamber

With a thrust of 25 tons, the V-2 motor was the world's first large, liquid-fuel rocket engine, and it powered the world's first ballistic missile, the German V-2 of World War II. This artifact, manufactured by Linke-Hofmann Werke AG, is cut away to show its internal mechanisms.

The combustion chamber, the engine's heart, burned the rocket's water alcohol and liquid oxygen propellants at about 2,700 °C (4,900 °F). The alcohol was injected through six pipes near the bottom of the chamber, moved up between the walls to cool the chamber, and emerged through the sides of the 18 injectors on top. Small pipes also injected alcohol into the chamber through rings of tiny holes to provide an insulating film of fuel along the walls. Liquid oxygen was injected directly into the top of the injector heads. A pyrotechnic igniter started combustion, after which burning was self-sustaining.

VEHICLE SPECIFICATIONS

Length:	1.96 m (6 ft 5 in)
Thrust:	245,000 N (56,000 lb)
Propellants:	liquid oxygen / 75 percent water alcohol
Manufacturer:	Linke-Hofmann Werke AG

Space Shuttle Main Engine

A cluster of three of these high-performance main engines provides the primary thrust to place the Space Shuttle orbiter into Earth orbit. These liquid-fuel engines burn for eight minutes and are reusable and throttleable. Two large, shorter-burning solid rocket boosters are also used during launch and are jettisoned after use. The main engines are serviced after each Shuttle flight and made ready for the next flight. On top of the engine's nozzle is the powerhead, which contains computers to regulate and monitor all engine functions.

ABOVE
A Space Shuttle Main Engine (SSME) undergoing a full power level 290.04 second test firing at the National Space Technology Laboratories (Stennis Space Center) in Mississippi. The firings were part of a series of developmental testing designed to increase the amount of thrust available to the Shuttle from its three main engines. The additional thrust allowed the Shuttle to launch heavier payloads into orbit.

ABOVE
Shuttle Main Engine on display

VEHICLE SPECIFICATIONS

Length:	4.2 m (14 ft)
Diameter, nozzle:	2.3 m (7.6 ft)
Weight:	3,008 kg (6,632 lb)
Thrust:	2,068,000 N (470,000 lb)
Propellants:	liquid oxygen and liquid hydrogen
Manufacturer:	Rocketdyne Div., Rockwell International Corp.

Goddard 1935 A-Series Rocket

This is probably the liquid-fuel rocket Robert H. Goddard tried to launch on September 23, 1935, at his facility in Roswell, New Mexico. He attempted to demonstrate its capabilities to supporters Charles Lindbergh and Harry Guggenheim. The Guggenheim Foundation for the Promotion of Aeronaautics funded Goddard's experiments in New Mexico.

A technical problem prevented the flight. But because earlier A series rocket launches had succeeded, both Lindbergh and Guggenheim felt Goddard was on the right track. Lindbergh persuaded Goddard to donate an A-series rocket to the Smithsonian, which he did in November 1935. Note the bundled parachute on the side.

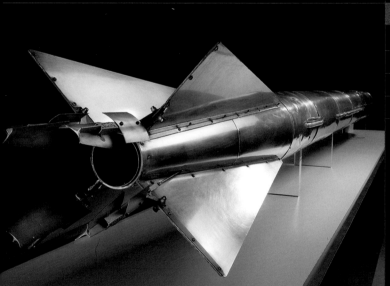

VEHICLE SPECIFICATIONS

Length:	4.7 m (15 ft 5 in)
Weight, loaded:	38 kg (85 lb)
Propellants:	gasoline, liquid oxygen
Builder:	Dr. Robert H. Goddard

TOP TO BOTTOM

The Goddard 1935 A-series rocket being placed into position for its attempted launch.

A view of the Goddard rocket fins and nozzle from the display at the Udvar-Hazy Center

The parachute pack can be seen near the top (image left) of the Goddard rocket.

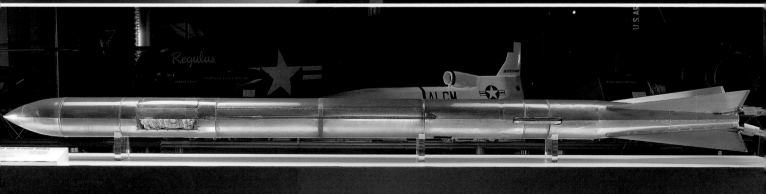

LEFT
Langley Aerodrome A just after leaving houseboat-mounted catapult and moments before crashing into the Potomac River on October 7, 1903.

BELOW
The Langley Aerodrome A has found a home, suspended at the Udvar-Hazy Center.

ABOVE
Manly-Balzer engine used on the Langley Aerodrome A

RIGHT
Langley Aerodrome A, being assembled on its launching platform.

Langley Aerodrome A

Samuel Langley's successful flights of model-size Aerodromes in 1896 led him to build a full-size, human-carrying airplane. Langley's simple approach was merely to scale up the unpiloted Aerodromes to human-carrying proportions, which proved to be a grave error. He focused primarily on the power plant. The completed engine, a water-cooled five-cylinder radial with remarkable power, was indeed a great achievement.

Despite the excellent engine, Langley's Aerodrome A met with disastrous results, crashing on takeoff on October 7, 1903, and again on December 8—only nine days before the Wright brothers' historic flights. While Langley blamed the launch mechanism, it is clear that the aircraft was overly complex, structurally weak, and aerodynamically unsound. The second crash ended Langley's aeronautical work.

AIRCRAFT SPECIFICATIONS

Wingspan:	14.8 m (48 ft 5 in)
Length:	16 m (52 ft 5 in)
Height:	3.5 m (11 ft 4 in)
Weight:	340 kg (750 lb) including pilot
Engine:	Manly-Balzer 5-cylinder radial, 52.4 hp
Builder:	Samuel P. Langley, Washington, D.C., 1903

TOP
The Langley Aerodrome A was rebuilt by Glenn Curtiss at Hammondsport, N.Y., in 1914. Among the many modifications made by Curtiss were new wings, the addition of floats, replacing the engine with a Curtiss V-8, and Curtiss-style controls. In this image, Curtiss Company pilot, Walter Johnson, flies the highly modified Langley Aerodrome A in 1914.

BOTTOM
The Langley Aerodrome A on exhibit in the Smithsonian's Arts and Industries Building after restoration to its original 1903 configuration by the Smithsonian in 1918.

TOP
The Fa 330 at the Paul E. Garber Restoration Facility's shop in 1975 prior to restoration

ABOVE LEFT
The restored aircraft is readied for shipment to the NASM mall location for display.

RIGHT
The Fa 330 underwent its initial submarine trials aboard *U523* in the Baltic Sea during August 1942.

Focke-Achgelis
Fa 330

This rotary-wing kite enabled World War II German submarines to locate targets in heavy seas. Simple to fly, the Fa 330 could be towed aloft as high as 220 meters (722 feet), where the pilot could sight as far as 53 kilometers (33 miles). He communicated his observations by a telephone line that ran along the tow cable. An ingenious parachute system allowed the pilot to escape from the aircraft at relatively low altitudes.

A crew of four could assemble or disassemble an Fa 330 in three minutes. When not in use, it remained stowed in two watertight tubes in the U-boat's conning tower. U-boat commanders disliked the aircraft—it gave away their submarine's location both visually and on radar. Only Type IX D2 U-boats operating in the Indian Ocean deployed them.

AIRCRAFT SPECIFICATIONS

Rotor diameter:	8.5 m (28 ft)
Length:	4.5 m (14 ft 8 in)
Height:	1.7 m (5 ft 6 in)
Weight, empty:	75 kg (165 lb)
Weight, gross:	175 kg (386 lb)
Top speed:	80 km/h (50 mph)
Manufacturer:	Weser Flugzeugbau, Hoykenkamp, Germany, 1944

TOP TO BOTTOM
The Fa 330 at the Udvar-Hazy Center

A close-up of the small instrument panel that was located between the pilot's feet

Spad XVI

The Spad XVI is a two-seat version of the highly successful, single-seat Spad fighters of World War I. It was introduced in January 1918. The first Spad two-seater design to see front-line service was the Spad XI. The Spad XVI was an attempt to improve upon the XI by upgrading the engine to a slightly more powerful Lorraine-Dietrich 8Bb. It was also a bit faster but had a lower ceiling and equally poor handling qualities, and thus offered no overall improvement. Nonetheless, about 1,000 Spad XVIs were built, and they ultimately equipped 32 French escadrilles.

This Spad XVI is significant because of its association with Brig. Gen. William "Billy" Mitchell, who piloted it on many observation flights over the front lines during pivotal battles in the last months of the war.

AIRCRAFT SPECIFICATIONS

Wingspan:	11.2 m (36 ft 9 in)
Length:	7.8 m (25 ft 7 in)
Height:	2.8 m (9 ft 2 in)
Weight, empty:	906 kg (1,994 lb)
Weight, gross:	1,140 kg (2,508 lb)
Top speed:	180 km/h (112 mph)
Engine:	Lorraine-Dietrich 8Bb, 240 hp
Armament:	one .30 cal. Vickers and two .30 cal. Lewis machine guns
Manufacturer:	Société Anonyme pour l'Aviation et ses Derives (SPAD)

TOP TO BOTTOM

The Spad XVI was a two-seat version of the very successful World War I French single-seat fighters, the Spad VII and the Spad XIII.

A wind-driven generator to provide electrical power on board the Spad XVI

Rear armament on the Spad XVI was twin Lewis machine guns on a pivoting mount.

Nieuport 28C.1

The **Nieuport 28C.1** was introduced in mid-1917 but was rejected by France in favor of the sturdier, more advanced Spad XIII. With no suitable fighter of its own, the United States adopted the Nieuport until France could provide the much-in-demand Spads. Nieuport 28s were the first aircraft to serve with an American fighter unit under U.S. command and in support of U.S. troops, and the first to score a victory with a U.S. unit.

The Nieuport 28 also made its mark after the war. The U.S. Navy used twelve for shipboard launching trials in 1919–21. The U.S. Army operated others in the 1920s. Several in private hands were modified for air racing, and some found their way into Hollywood movies. Still others became privately owned and flew in sporting and commercial capacities. This airplane contains components from as many as five Nieuport 28s.

AIRCRAFT SPECIFICATIONS

Wingspan:	8.2 m (26 ft 11 in)
Length:	6.5 m (21 ft 4 in)
Height:	2.5 m (8 ft 2 in)
Weight, empty:	533 kg (1,173 lb)
Weight, gross:	737 kg (1,625 lb)
Top speed:	200 km/h (124 mph)
Engine:	Gnôme Monosoupape 9N rotary, 160 hp
Armament:	two .30 cal. Vickers aircraft machine guns
Manufacturer:	Société Anonyme des Éstablissements Nieuport, Issy-les-Moulineaux, France, 1918

TOP TO BOTTOM

Lineup of Nieuport 28s during the making of the Hollywood film *The Dawn Patrol* in 1938. Film stars Errol Flynn and David Niven are in the first two aircraft.

The Nieuport 28C.1 awaits final placement at the Udvar-Hazy Center. The sleek SR-71 Blackbird provides a remarkable background for this WW I fighter.

Lt. James A. Meissner of the U.S. Air Service's famous "Hat-in-the-Ring" 94th Aero Squadron, wearing his newly awarded Croix de Guerre, May 15, 1918. NASM's Nieuport 28 was finished in the colors of Meissner's aircraft.

Caudron G.4

Although World War I fighter aircraft often command greater attention, the most influential role of aviation in the war was reconnaissance. An early light bomber and reconnaissance aircraft, the French Caudron G.4 was a principal type used when these critical air power roles were being conceived and pioneered.

The extensive deployment of the Caudron G.4 for reconnaissance during World War I makes it an especially important early military aircraft. Despite its speed and armament limitations, the G.4 was quite reliable, had a good rate of climb, and was pleasant to fly—characteristics that also made it a good training aircraft. Many Allied pilots received their initial flight training in G.4s. This one is among the oldest surviving bombers in the world, and one of the very few remaining multi-engine aircraft from WWI.

AIRCRAFT SPECIFICATIONS

Wingspan:	17.2 m (56 ft 5 in)
Length:	7.2 m (23 ft 8 in)
Height:	2.6 m (8 ft 6 in)
Weight, empty:	733 kg (1,616 lb)
Weight, gross:	1,232 kg (2,716 lb)
Top speed:	132 km/h (82 mph)
Engines:	two Le Rhône 9C, 80 hp
Armament:	two .30 caliber Lewis machine guns
Manufacturer:	Caudron Frères, Issy-les-Moulineaux, France, 1916

TOP TO BOTTOM
Caudron G.4 in flight

Caudron G.4 of French Escadrille C.11 on February 26, 1917

In its location at the Hazy Center, this view from the rear through the tail of the G.4 provides a unique perspective to the Caudron's construction.

BELOW
Artistic butterfly nose art on a Caudron G.4 of the Franco-Belgian Escadrille C.74

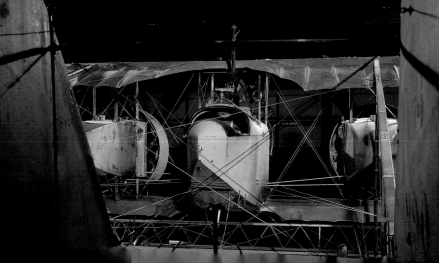

TOP
The NASM Caudron G.4 on display in building #21 at the Garber Restoration Facility awaiting preservation

BOTTOM LEFT
Caudron G.4 in flight at Issy-les-Moulineaux, site of the Caudron Factory

BOTTOM RIGHT
Caudron G.4 in Dutch markings, with orange national insignia on white rudder

RIGHT AND BELOW
The Garber team details the interior and wing of the L-5. Beautiful wood structures and a simple cockpit design are only visible during a full restoration. The L-5 was the last complete aircraft restoration accomplished at the Paul E. Garber Restoration Facility before the move to the Udvar-Hazy Center.

Stinson L-5 Sentinel

Versatile, durable, and an important aircraft of World War II, the L-5 flew a wide variety of missions: photo reconnaissance, resupply, evacuation of wounded, message courier, VIP transport, and artillery spotting. Its design was roughly derived from the prewar Stinson Model 105 Voyager. The Army Air Corps purchased six Voyagers from Vultee Aircraft (which had acquired Stinson) in 1941 for testing. Refitted with the Lycoming O-435-1 engine, the aircraft was designated the Model 75. While it had features and components of the Voyager series, it was fundamentally a new design.

The Army ordered this model in quantity, designating it first as the O-62 ("O" for observation), then as the L-5 ("L" for liaison) when the type designation was changed in 1942. This aircraft was the first O-62/L-5 produced.

AIRCRAFT SPECIFICATIONS

Wingspan:	10.4 m (34 ft)
Length:	7.3 m (24 ft 1 in)
Height:	2.1 m (7 ft 1 in)
Weight, empty:	703 kg (1,550 lb)
Weight, gross:	916 kg (2,020 lb)
Top speed:	185 km/h (115 mph)
Engine:	Lycoming O-435-1, horizontally opposed 6-cylinder, 185 hp
Crew:	2
Manufacturer:	Consolidated Vultee, Stinson Div., Wayne, Mich., 1942

ABOVE
An L-4 in the "Brodie" configuration prepares for takeoff. This unique launch and recovery system allowed the aircraft to penetrate austere locations by launching from mobile small ships or even by "landing" in rough terrain on a tightrope-like wire system.

NASM's aircraft is the first production model of the L–5—originally numbered the O–62. The "L" stood for "Liaison" while the "O" stood for "Observation."

The innovative "Brodie" system is incorporated into the display of the L–5 at the Udvar–Hazy Center.

Apollo Extravehicular Gloves
These gloves were developmental versions of those later worn on the lunar surface.

Lunar EVA Artifacts

THESE OBJECTS ARE EXAMPLES of personal equipment and tools issued to astronauts of the Mercury, Gemini, and Apollo programs. Some of the objects were used in training for missions, others during the actual missions. They include items of protective clothing (gloves, helmets, and boots), a spacesuit worn on the Moon, and examples of the types of tools astronauts used on the lunar surface. The actual tools used on the Moon were left behind.

Small Artifacts

TOP
This "short snorter" signed by many military aviation notables, Hap Arnold and Jimmy Doolittle to name a few, was carried by aviators who had flown across the vast reaches of ocean to frequently remote locations.

BELOW LEFT AND RIGHT

Nazi Swastika
Taken as a war trophy, this Nazi symbol—the swastika—was cut from a German glider.

Japanese Flag
It was tradition for the family of any Japanese citizen who was called to service to write messages of encouragement on a flag or sash that would be carried into battle for luck and protection.

THROUGHOUT AMERICA'S HANGAR there are displayed more than just air and spacecraft. Significant artifacts representing the history of aviation fill a number of exhibit cases related to a variety of topics—from sport aviation to the most modern military advances yet witnessed. Objects representing not only America's aviation experiences but also many spectacular fragments of history from around the globe help to expose some of the personal side of a very technologically oriented subject. The NASM small artifact collection contains more than 50,000 objects.

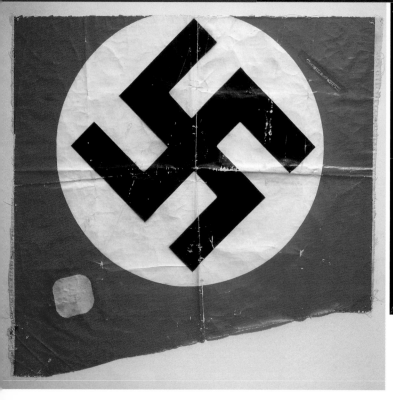

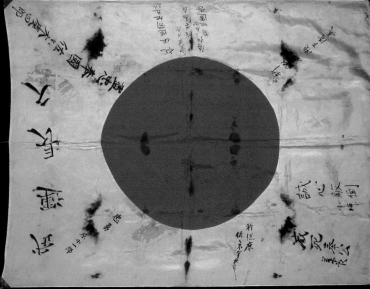

OPPOSITE TOP LEFT
General Curtis E. LeMay's service cap

OPPOSITE TOP RIGHT
Several World War II leather jackets are on display featuring traditional artwork. Behind these jackets is General Hap Arnold's 5-star flag. Arnold directed that one of each type of WWII aircraft be preserved for all time. The richness of the NASM military collection has its roots in Arnold's orders.

B-17 Bomber crew hat
Attitude indicator from the B-24 *Lady Be Good*
Arming plugs from the *Little Boy* atomic bomb
A bolt cut from Jimmy Doolittle's B-25 after the Tokyo Raid

TOP LEFT
Medals earned by Lafayette Escadrille pilot Edwin C. Parsons

TOP RIGHT
World War I shell casing brass artwork

BOTTOM LEFT
Artifacts from the 9/11 attacks on the World Trade Center and the Pentagon

BOTTOM RIGHT
A North Vietnamese rocket launcher
Viet Cong sandals
"Dog Doo" transmitter used by the CIA to monitor movement on the Ho Chi Minh trail

Reconnaissance Party Suits

(left) Worn by an RF-4C pilot, this "Rhino" driver
(another name for any F-4 crewman) trained for low
altitude tactical missions throughout the Pacific during
the Cold War.

(right) Worn by an SR-71 Pilot, the HABU patch indicates
that this pilot has flown operational strategic reconnaissance missions.

Charles A. Lindbergh and the Stanley King Collection

ON MAY 20-21, 1927, Charles A. Lindbergh literally flew into history when he crossed the Atlantic Ocean in his Ryan NY-P *Spirit of St. Louis,* thus becoming the first pilot to fly solo and nonstop from New York to Paris. This flight made Lindbergh a household name and catapulted him into fame and celebrity.

These artifacts are representative of the National Air and Space Museum's collection of materials that Lindbergh took with him on his numerous and historic flights. These include the *Spirit*'s transatlantic crossing and its other significant flights throughout the 48 states in 1927 as well as those into Latin America and the Caribbean in 1927 and 1928. They also comprise the great circle route flight to the Orient in 1931, and the exploratory flight from Newfoundland via Greenland to Europe for Pan American World Airways in 1933 in the Lockheed Sirius *Tingmissartoq,* made with Anne Morrow Lindbergh.

The objects of popular culture surrounding the core display—everything from ashtrays to wristwatches—are typical of the public adulation for Lindbergh, but more especially of the powerful commercial response to his celebrity. More than seventy-five years after the historic flight of the *Spirit,* Lindbergh's name still has the power to create a market for manufactured goods that are designed to make a profit from his fame.

These items of Lindbergh memorabilia were collected by Stanley King of New York City and donated by him to the National Air and Space Museum in 2002.

ABOVE
Medallion with map of trans-Atlantic flight

RIGHT
Bottle of quinine tablets from Lindbergh's survival kit

BELOW
Toys, models

LEFT
Boot, letter from Lindbergh, commemorative watches and clocks, cuff links, doll

ABOVE
Whirling airplane toy, train car, truck, magnetic game

BELOW
Slide rule, compass, penlight

Lockheed SR-71A Blackbird

RIGHT (BACKGROUND)
Captain "Buck" Adams gives a spirited thumbs-up before departing with his RSO, Major William "Bill" Machorek, from London on another Blackbird record-setting flight. On September 13, 1974, this SR-71 flew from London to Los Angeles in about 4 hours.

ABOVE
After flying from Los Angeles to Washington, D.C., in 1 hour and 4 minutes, this SR-71 landed at Dulles International Airport and was transferred to the nation's aircraft collection.

BELOW
The National Air and Space Museum's SR-71A was also flown by U.S. Air Force Colonel Tom Alison (left), who became the Museum's Chief of the Collections Division. Flying with Detachment 1 at Kadena Air Force Base, Okinawa, Alison logged many sorties in this airplane. Also shown here is Alison's paired "backseater," Joseph "J. T." Vida, who had flown more hours in SR-71s than any other crewmember when the Blackbird was retired from service.

No reconnaissance aircraft in history has operated globally in more hostile airspace or with such complete impunity than the SR-71, the world's fastest jet-propelled aircraft. The Blackbird's performance and operational achievements placed it at the pinnacle of aviation technology developments during the Cold War.

This Blackbird accrued about 2,800 hours of flight time during 24 years of active service with the U.S. Air Force. On its last flight, March 6, 1990, Lt. Col. Ed Yeilding and Lt. Col. Joseph Vida set a speed record by flying from Los Angeles to Washington, D.C., in 1 hour, 4 minutes, 20 seconds, averaging 3,418 kilometers (2,124 miles) per hour. At the flight's conclusion, they landed at Washington Dulles International Airport and turned the airplane over to the Smithsonian.

AIRCRAFT SPECIFICATIONS

Wingspan:	16.9 m (55 ft 7 in)
Length:	32.7 m (107 ft 5 in)
Height:	5.6 m (18 ft 6 in)
Weight, empty:	27,216 kg (60,000 lb)
Weight, gross:	63,504 kg (140,000 lb)
Top speed:	3,620 km/h (2,250 mph), Mach 3.3
Engines:	two Pratt & Whitney J-58 (JT11D-20B), 15,422 kg (34,000 lb) thrust
Crew:	2
Manufacturer:	Lockheed Aircraft Corp., Palmdale, Calif., 1967

ABOVE
The SR-71 bridged the gap between aircraft and spacecraft. The fastest manned aircraft ever built, all Blackbirds were finally grounded in 1999 because they became too expensive to operate. Orbiting satellites now provide the data that Blackbirds once collected.

BOTTOM LEFT
The Blackbird's cockpit was a tight fit for the crew, who wore bulky pressure suits during each mission.

BOTTOM RIGHT
The Blackbird was built for speed—Mach 3 plus. It was the Corvette of modern aircraft and is still the fastest aircraft ever built.

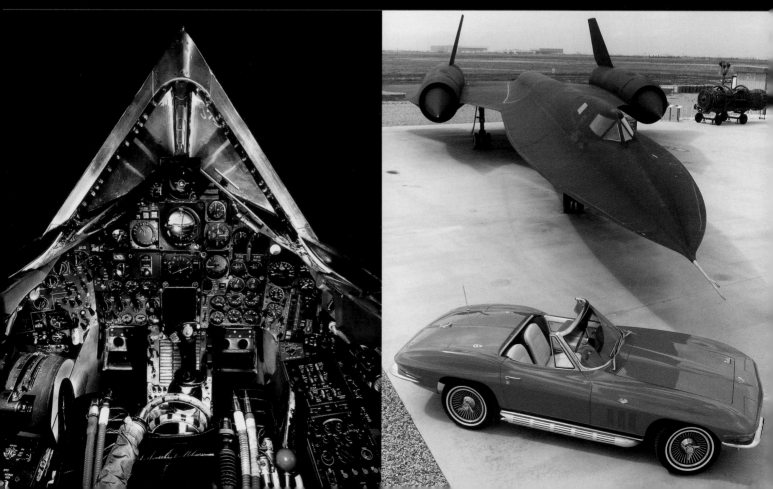

Lockheed Martin X-35B STOVL Joint Strike Fighter

The Joint Strike Fighter is a stealthy, supersonic, multi-role fighter. Three versions are planned. The conventional takeoff and landing variant, designed for the U.S. Air Force, will be built in the largest quantities. The U.S. Navy's carrier variant features larger wing and control surfaces, additional wingtip ailerons, and a special structure to absorb punishing catapult launches and arrested landings. The short takeoff/vertical landing version has a unique shaft-driven, lift-fan propulsion system that enables the aircraft to take off from a very short runway or small aircraft carrier and land vertically.

This first X-35 ever built was modified to include the lift-fan engine. It was the first aircraft in history to achieve a short takeoff, level supersonic dash, and vertical landing in a single flight, and the first to fly using the shaft-driven, lift-fan propulsion system.

ABOVE
The X-35 test program was one of the shortest and most successful in aviation history. The X-35B will replace the AV-8B Harrier, among other aging jet platforms. It will be flown by the U.S. Marine Corps and the air forces of Great Britain.

BELOW
The X-35B astonished former military fliers during the Salute to Veterans held at the Udvar-Hazy Center on December 9, 2003.

AIRCRAFT SPECIFICATIONS

Wingspan:	10 m (33 ft)
Length:	15.47 m (50 ft 9 in)
Height:	5 m (15 ft)
Weight:	15,876 kg (35,000 lb)
Engine:	one Pratt & Whitney JSF119-PW-611 turbofan, total vertical lift 164.6 kN (37,000 lb)
Crew:	1
Armament:	internal cannon
Ordnance:	two AIM-120 air-to-air missiles and two 1,000-lb precision-guided bombs
Manufacturer:	Lockheed Martin, Palmdale, Calif., 2001

The NASM X-35B STOVL was the first aircraft in history to accomplish a short takeoff, supersonic run, and vertical landing on the same mission.

BELOW LEFT AND RIGHT
Testing the Pratt & Whitney JSF119-PW-611 turbofan on the engine test stand at night provided some spectacular views.

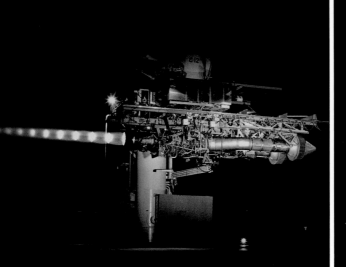

McDonnell F-4S Phantom II

The U.S. Air Force, Navy, and Marine Corps and air forces of twelve other nations have flown the multi-role Phantom II. In this aircraft, then a Navy F-4J, on June 21, 1972, Cmdr. S. C. Flynn and his radar intercept officer, Lt. W. H. John, spotted three enemy MiG fighters off the coast of Vietnam and shot down one MiG-21 with a Sidewinder air-to-air missile. This Phantom also flew combat air patrols and bombing missions during the Linebacker II bombing campaign that same year.

Later assigned to the Marine Corps, this F-4J was extensively modernized and designated an F-4S. Changes included improving the engines (smokeless), hydraulics, electronics, and wiring; modifying the wings to increase maneuverability; and adding a radar homing and warning antenna, as well as formation tape lights on the fuselage and vertical tail.

AIRCRAFT SPECIFICATIONS

Wingspan:	11.6 m (38 ft 5 in)
Length:	17.7 m (58 ft 3 in)
Height:	5 m (17 ft 4 in)
Weight, empty:	13,960 kg (30,780 lb)
Weight, gross:	23,250 kg (51,300 lb)
Top speed:	2,298 km/h (1,428 mph), Mach 2.2
Engines:	two General Electric J79-GE-10 turbojets, 8,119 kg (17,900 lb) thrust
Crew:	2
Ordnance:	four AIM-7 Sparrow and four AIM-9 Sidewinder air-to-air missiles, 7,257-kg (16,000-lb) bomb load
Manufacturer:	McDonnell Douglas Corp., St. Louis, Mo., 1970

TOP LEFT
The F-4, still a "J" model, lands on the USS *Saratoga*.

RIGHT
This APG-59 radar was part of the solid-state AN/AWG-10 Missile Control System used in many Navy F-4 aircraft.

Flag of the Republic of Vietnam

Both of these flags from the Vietnam War are part of the NASM collection.

Flag of the Viet Cong (People's Liberation Forces in South Vietnam)

ABOVE
Here the NASM F-4S is displayed with an AIM-9 heat-seeking missile nearby.

BELOW
Graphic artist Jim Qualls has created this portrait of NASM's F-4S Phantom II in its Navy colors.

Gliders

Grob 102
Standard Astir III

On February 17, 1986, a tow plane hauled Robert Harris and this Grob 102 sailplane aloft over central California. He unhooked the towline and skillfully climbed to an altitude of 10,640 meters (35,000 feet). Strong air currents then lifted the glider up at a rate of 182–243 meters (600–800 feet) per minute. At 12,768 meters (42,000 feet), Harris's eyes began to water, and his teardrops immediately froze and formed ice cobwebs. Even five layers of clothing could not insulate him from temperatures that dropped to -50°C (-58°F) inside the cockpit. A failing oxygen system forced him to stop his climb at 14,899 meters (49,009 feet), and he returned triumphantly to earth using backup oxygen. This world sailplane altitude record bettered the old mark by more than 821 meters (2,700 feet).

AIRCRAFT SPECIFICATIONS

Wingspan:	15 m (49 ft 2 in)
Length:	6.7 m (22 ft)
Height:	1.3 m (4 ft 1 in)
Weight, empty:	255 kg (562 lb)
Weight, gross:	450 kg (992 lb)
Top glide speed:	92 km/h (57 mph)
Manufacturer:	Burkhart Grob Flugzeug GmbH & Co. KG, Mindelheim-Mattsies Airfield, Germany, 1981

Bowlus BA-100
Baby Albatross

The Baby Albatross, designed by William Hawley Bowlus, became one of the most successful kit-built sailplanes. In 1938, Bowlus began selling kits that included all the essential parts for building the aircraft. A complete Baby Albatross kit could be bought for less than one-third the price of other ready-to-fly sailplanes. Pilots built more than 50 of them. The start of World War II ended sales, but Bowlus succeeded in making soaring more accessible by offering this attractive kit airplane.

AIRCRAFT SPECIFICATIONS

Wingspan:	13.6 m (44 ft 6 in)
Length:	5.8 m (18 ft 11 in)
Weight, empty:	140 kg (312 lb)
Weight, gross:	229 kg (505 lb)
Manufacturer:	Bowlus Sailplanes, Inc., San Fernando, Calif.

Bowlus 1-S-2100
Senior Albatross *Falcon*

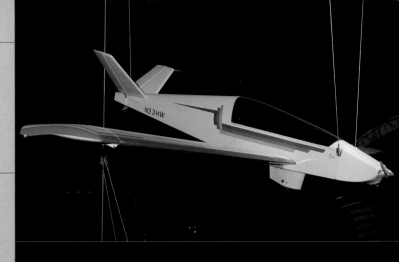

Hawley Bowlus developed the Senior Albatross series in 1933 from a design he called the Bowlus Super Sailplane. Bowlus was influenced by German designers and pilots who then led the world in building and flying high-performance gliders. Warren E. Eaton acquired this sailplane from Bowlus in 1934. Eaton had flown Spad XIII fighters for the U.S. Army Air Service's 103rd Aero Squadron at Issoudon, France, and was credited with downing one enemy aircraft. After the war, Eaton founded the Soaring Society of America and became that organization's first president.

AIRCRAFT SPECIFICATIONS

Wingspan:	18.8 m (61 ft 9 in)
Length:	7.2 m (23 ft 7 in)
Height:	1.6 m (5 ft 4 in)
Weight, empty:	154 kg (340 lb)
Weight, gross:	236 kg (520 lb)
Top glide speed:	55 km/h (34 mph)
Manufacturer:	Bowlus-du Pont Sailplane Co., San Fernando, Calif., 1934

Monnett Moni

Schoolteacher John Monnett designed the Moni during the early 1980s, and then coined the term "air recreation vehicle" to describe it. Monnett's design captured many of the merits that leisure pilots sought in one aircraft. The Moni looked great, performed well, and was reasonably simple to construct in one's own garage. Harold C. Weston built this one and flew it more than 40 hours, before donating it to the Smithsonian in 1992.

AIRCRAFT SPECIFICATIONS

Wingspan:	8.4 m (27 ft 6 in)
Length:	4.5 m (14 ft 7½ in)
Height:	0.7 m (28 in)
Weight, empty:	118 kg (260 lb)
Weight, gross:	227 kg (500 lb)
Top speed:	193 km/h (120 mph)
Engine:	KFM 107E, 2-cylinder, 2-stroke, air-cooled, 25 hp
Kit manufacturer:	Monnett Experimental Aircraft
Builder:	Harold C. Weston, 1989

Mikoyan-Gurevich
MiG-15bis "Fagot B"

ABOVE LEFT
On the morning of March 5, 1953, Lt. Franciszek Jarecki defected from the Polish Air Force while leading a patrol of four MiG-15s from his base at Stolp, Poland. He wore this flight suit during his daring flight to freedom.

ABOVE RIGHT
The MiG-15 usually flew near the North Korea/China border in an area known as MiG Alley.

Arch rival to the U.S. F-86 in Korea, the MiG-15 shocked the West with its capabilities. The Soviets designed the aircraft in 1946 to answer an urgent need for a high-altitude day interceptor. It first flew in late 1947. The MiG-15 was the first Soviet jet to benefit from the British sale to Russia of the new Rolls Royce Nene and Derwent jet engines, which the Soviets immediately copied and refined. The resulting RD-500, Klimov RD-45, and modified VK-1 engines gave a powerful boost to Soviet jet technology.

The MiG-15 featured the first production swept wing, pressurized cockpit, and ejection seat on a Soviet aircraft. Although Mikoyan and Gurevich were aware of German turbojet and swept-wing work, this design was wholly Russian, except for the engine. The NASM's MiG-15bis is a Chinese Ji-2 modification.

AIRCRAFT SPECIFICATIONS

Wingspan:	10.1 m (33 ft 2 in)
Length:	10.1 m (33 ft 2 in)
Height:	3.4 m (10 ft 10 in)
Weight, empty:	3,523 kg (7,767 lb)
Weight, gross:	5,405 kg (11,916 lb)
Top speed:	1,050 km/h (652 mph)
Engine:	RD-45F centrifugal-flow turbojet, 2,270 kg (4,994 lb) thrust
Armament:	one 30 mm and two 23 mm cannons
Manufacturer:	Mikoyan-Gurevich, late 1940s

Mikoyan-Gurevich
MiG-21F "Fishbed C"

The MiG-21 was the Soviet Union's first truly modern, second-generation jet fighter. Testing began in 1956, and the first version entered service in 1960 as the MiG-21F-13. Soviet designers developed a unique "tailed delta" configuration with a very thin delta wing, which gave the aircraft maneuverability, high speed, good medium-altitude performance, and adequate takeoff and landing characteristics.

The MiG-21 became the standard Soviet clear-air interceptor. With the addition of radar, a more powerful engine, and other modifications, it became a multi-role fighter. More than 6,000 MiG-21s of 12 types were flown by over three dozen nations.

AIRCRAFT SPECIFICATIONS

Wingspan:	7.2 m (23 ft 6 in)
Length:	15.8 m (51 ft 8 in)
Height:	4.1 m (13 ft 2 in)
Weight, empty:	4,871 kg (10,739 lb)
Weight, gross:	8,625 kg (19,015 lb)
Top speed:	2,175 km/h (1,352 mph), Mach 2.04
Engine:	R-11F-300 axial-flow turbojet, 5,740 kg (12,655 lb) thrust
Armament:	23 mm GSh-23L two-barrel cannon
Ordnance:	two K-13/AA-2 Atoll or R-60/AA-8 Aphid air-to-air missiles or two 500-kg bombs
Manufacturer:	Mikoyan-Gurevich, early 1960s

During the Cold War, the MiG-21 characterized the Soviet tendency to rely upon simple technology and superior numbers.

Bell UH-1H Iroquois "Huey"

The Huey with its characteristic "Whop, Whop, Whop" sound was the icon of the War in Southeast Asia—Vietnam.

In 1956 the Iroquois, commonly known as the Huey, first flew as an Army replacement for the H-13 medevac helicopter of Korean War fame. By the end of the century, Bell and its licensees had produced more Hueys than any other American military aircraft, except for the Consolidated B-24. Superbly suited to air mobility and medical evacuation missions in Vietnam, the Huey became the icon of that conflict. This UH-1 compiled a distinguished combat record in Vietnam from 1966 to 1970. Numerous patches on its skin attest to the ferocity of missions flown with the 229th Assault Helicopter Battalion of the 1st Cavalry, the 118th and 128th Assault Helicopter Companies, and the 11th Combat Aviation Battalion.

AIRCRAFT SPECIFICATIONS

Rotor diameter:	14.7 m (48 ft 3 in)
Length:	12.6 m (41 ft 5 in)
Height:	4.2 m (13 ft 7 in)
Weight, empty:	2,580 kg (5,687 lb)
Weight, gross:	4,309 kg (9,500 lb)
Top speed:	222 km/h (138 mph)
Engine:	Lycoming T53-L-13BA, 1,400 shp
Crew:	4
Armament:	4 M-60 machine guns (smoke ship)
Manufacturer:	Bell Helicopter, Fort Worth, Tex., 1966

Bell XV-15
Tilt Rotor
Research Aircraft

The XV-15 Tilt Rotor hovers during its final approach to land just outside the Udvar-Hazy Center.

The XV-15 Tilt Rotor technology demonstrator was the culmination of efforts begun in the early 1950s to produce an aircraft that could take off, land, and hover like a helicopter, but could fly with the speed of an airplane. The rotor pylons tilt from vertical to horizontal, to eliminate the speed barriers that impact conventional helicopters. This is the second of two XV-15s built by Bell under a joint NASA/Army program. From 1979 to 2003, it logged 700 hours in testing and demonstrated operations under a wide range of conditions. Its success encouraged Bell and the Marine Corps to develop the scaled-up MV-22 Osprey as a replacement for Marine transport helicopters.

AIRCRAFT SPECIFICATIONS

Wingspan:	9.8 m (32 ft 2 in)
Proprotor diameter:	7.6 m (25 ft)
Length:	12.8 m (42 ft 1 in)
Height:	3.9 m (12 ft 8 in)
Weight, empty:	4,574 kg (10,083 lb)
Weight, gross:	6,009 kg (13,248 lb)
Top speed:	550 km/h (342 mph)
Engine:	2 Lycoming LTC1K-41K turboshafts (modified T53), 1,550 shp
Crew:	2
Manufacturer:	Bell Helicopter, 1979

Vought-Sikorsky
XR-4C

This artifact was the original XR-4 and was later redesignated with a "C" due to improvements made after its initial testing.

The XR-4 served as the prototype for the world's first mass-produced helicopter. It made its first flight six weeks after the United States entered World War II. The XR-4 quickly broke many helicopter records, including a 1,225-kilometer (761-mile) flight from Bridgeport, Connecticut, to Wright Field, Ohio, where it became the first helicopter to enter service with the U.S. military. By late 1943, it had completed its mission to prove the value of the helicopter in military service.

Sikorsky produced 130 R-4 helicopters, 55 of which went to the Army Air Forces, 23 to the Coast Guard and Navy, and 52 to Great Britain. The Army Air Forces mainly used the R-4 as a trainer, but 20 R-4s served in the Pacific and Burma theaters during the last 16 months of the war. They performed liaison and rescue duties, including the first medical evacuations by helicopter.

AIRCRAFT SPECIFICATIONS

Rotor diameter:	11.6 m (38 ft)
Length:	10.7 m (35 ft)
Height:	3.6 m (11 ft 11 in)
Weight, empty:	912 kg (2,010 lb)
Weight, gross:	1,148 kg (2,540 lb)
Top speed:	134 km/h (83 mph)
Engine:	Warner R-550-1 Super Scarab, 200 hp
Manufacturer:	Vought-Sikorsky Div., United Aircraft Corp., Stratford, Conn., 1942

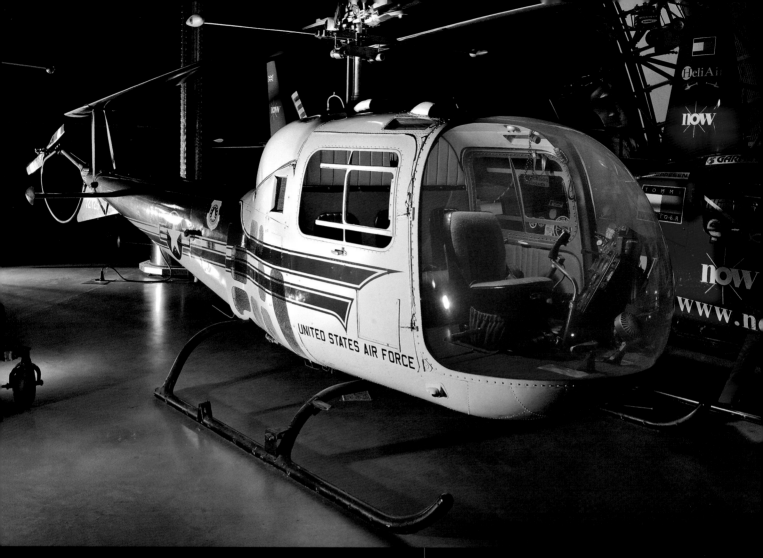

Bell H-13J

The Air Force retired both of the former Presidential transport H-13J's in 1967 and transferred one of the helicopters to the Air and Space Museum in 1968.

Dwight D. Eisenhower became the first U.S. president to fly aboard a helicopter in this U.S. Air Force H-13J on July 12, 1957. It was one of two modified H-13Js the Air Force purchased for evacuating the President to a remote command post in the event of a military confrontation with the Soviet Union. The H-13J also shuttled President Eisenhower to Washington's National Airport and his personal retreat in Gettysburg, Pennsylvania. Larger, more comfortable models soon replaced it in presidential transport duties.

Sold commercially as the Model 47, the H-13J was a direct evolution of Bell's first helicopter, the Model 30. On the "J" models, known as "Rangers," Bell increased the seating from two to four by stretching the cabin and relocating the instrument panel to the left side of the pilot's seat.

AIRCRAFT SPECIFICATIONS

Rotor diameter:	11.3 m (37 ft 2 in)
Length:	9.9 m (32 ft 5 in)
Height:	2.9 m (9 ft 4 in)
Weight, empty:	862 kg (1,900 lb)
Weight, gross:	1,293 kg (2,850 lb)
Top speed:	169 km/h (105 mph)
Engine:	Lycoming VO-435-A1B, 260 hp, de-rated to 220 hp
Manufacturer:	Bell Helicopters Corp., Fort Worth, Tex., 1957

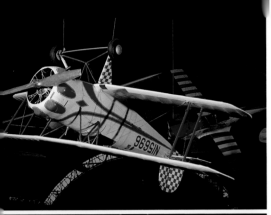

The Boeing Aviation Hangar features aircraft hanging at several levels, suspended from the building's huge trusses, and aircraft displayed on the hangar floor. The suspended aircraft have been hung at various angles to demonstrate typical flight maneuvers. Visitors will see an aerobatic airplane suspended upside down, a World War II fighter angling for a victory and a small two-seater flying level. Multi-level walkways rising about four stories above the floor provide a wide variety of angles from which to view the aircraft and spacecraft on display.

Aerobatic, general aviation, commercial and World War I and II aircraft are located to the south of the entry ramp. To the north, visitors encounter the post–World War II military aircraft collection including Russian MiGs, carrier aircraft, military helicopters, and land-based fighters. One of the most memorable vistas, the entryway overlook, provides an opportunity to view the sleek Lockheed SR-71 Blackbird, the fastest airplane ever built, from the front and above—much like it would be seen during midair refueling.

The Boeing Aviation Hangar is named in honor of the Boeing Company, whose generous support of the Museum's Steven F. Udvar-Hazy Center will help to complete a new restoration facility and archives.

James S. McDonnell Space Hangar

During a visit to the National Air and Space Museum's Steven F. Udvar-Hazy Center everyone can now explore the remarkable holdings in the James S. McDonnell Space Hangar. Opened in December 2004, the 53,000-square-foot Space Hangar features hundreds of space artifacts arrayed around its centerpiece, the Space Shuttle *Enterprise*. Objects range from the 69-foot floor-to-ceiling Redstone missile to tiny "Anita," a spider carried on Skylab for web formation experiments. The hangar and its holdings illustrate the scope of space exploration history as organized around four main themes: rocketry and missiles, human spaceflight, application satellites and space science.

More than 110 large space artifacts are housed in the hangar. The biggest and heaviest—including *Enterprise*, an instrument ring segment of a Saturn V rocket that was never built, and a Space Shuttle main engine—are displayed at ground level. An array of cruise missiles, satellites and space telescopes hangs from above. Two elevated overlooks allow visitors to study suspended artifacts straight-on and ground-level displays from above.

The McDonnell Space Hangar is named for aerospace pioneer James S. McDonnell, whose company built a number of pioneering aircraft and both the Mercury and Gemini spacecraft, flown by the first American astronauts.

Space Shuttle
Enterprise

The first Space Shuttle orbiter, *Enterprise* is a full-scale test vehicle used for flights in the atmosphere and tests on the ground. Officially designated Orbiter Vehicle 101 (OV-101), *Enterprise* is not equipped for spaceflight. It has no propulsion systems and only simulated thermal tiles.

In 1977 *Enterprise* completed approach and landing tests at NASA's Dryden Flight Research Center in California. It was flown atop a Boeing 747 carrier airplane and also released for piloted descents to check out its systems and performance. It later underwent launch vibration tests and fit checks at other NASA centers. Although *Enterprise* never flew in space, it introduced a new era in space transportation and was the flagship for a fleet of reusable shuttles. The Smithsonian acquired *Enterprise* in 1985.

VEHICLE SPECIFICATIONS

Wingspan:	24 m (78 ft)
Length:	37 m (122 ft)
Height:	17 m (57 ft)
Weight:	68,000 kg (150,000 lb)
Manufacturer:	Rockwell International (prime contractor)

TOP
The Shuttle's right side wing leading edge was used by NASA during evaluations following the *Columbia* disaster and is missing in this image.

LEFT TO RIGHT
View from directly astern, the shuttle tail towers above visitors at the Udvar-Hazy Center.

Restoration specialists prepare the cargo bay for painting.

A Manned Maneuvering Unit (MMU) is suspended above the *Enterprise* cockpit.

TOP
Enterprise rests patiently in temporary storage at Dulles International Airport surrounded by many other air and space artifacts.

BOTTOM LEFT
Rollout of *Enterprise* at Rockwell, the vehicle's manufacturer, in 1976

BOTTOM CENTER
Actors from the television series *Star Trek* join the festivities at the rollout ceremony.

BOTTOM RIGHT
The *Enterprise* test crews and the OV-101 test shuttle. Only two crewmen were on board during each test flight.

OPPOSITE TOP LEFT
The James S. McDonnell Space Hangar (shown under construction) houses *Enterprise* and many other historic space artifacts.

OPPOSITE CENTER LEFT
Enterprise separates from the 747 that carried the shuttle to altitude for glide testing.

OPPOSITE BOTTOM LEFT
A shuttle cockpit in the original configuration, before "glass cockpit" upgrades

OPPOSITE BOTTOM RIGHT
Successful completion of a glide test is celebrated by a unique flyby combination of T-38 chase planes and the 747 carrier aircraft.

OPPOSITE TOP RIGHT
The shuttle *Enterprise* being hoisted into position for vibration tests at NASA Marshall Space Flight Center in Alabama.

OPPOSITE CENTER RIGHT
Enterprise undergoes a "fit check" with the large liquid propellant tank and the twin solid rocket boosters on the launch pad at Kennedy Space Center in Florida.

APPROACH AND LANDING TEST

HAISE · FULLERTON   ENGLE · TRULY

USA

Enterprise

Mobile Quarantine Facility (Apollo 11)

This Mobile Quarantine Facility (MQF) was one of four built by NASA for astronauts returning from the Moon. Its purpose was to prevent the unlikely spread of lunar contagions by isolating the astronauts from contact with other people. A converted Airstream trailer, the MQF contained living and sleeping quarters, a kitchen, and a bathroom. Quarantine was assured by keeping the air pressure inside lower than the pressure outside and by filtering the air vented from the facility.

This MQF was used by Apollo 11 astronauts Armstrong, Aldrin, and Collins immediately after their return to Earth. They remained in it for 65 hours, while the MQF was flown from the aircraft carrier *Hornet* to a quarantine facility at the Johnson Space Center in Houston. They were allowed to emerge once scientists were sure they were not infected with "moon germs."

TOP TO BOTTOM

Apollo 11 astronaut Buzz Aldrin near the American flag on the moon's surface

Neil Armstrong, the first man to set foot on the moon, and Aldrin were monitored by a camera high atop the Lunar Excursion Module (LEM).

The Mobile Quarantine Facility (MQF) was carried on the aircraft carrier USS *Hornet*.

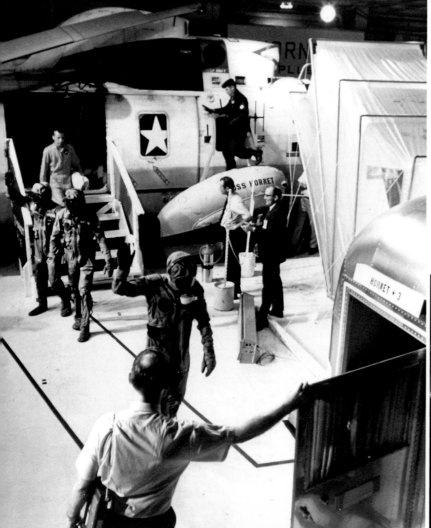

After splashdown, the astronauts don protective suits and then head for quarantine in the MQF.

Apollo 11 crew inside the MQF, Astronaut Michael Collins (left), the command module pilot, became the first Director of the National Air and Space Museum.

First visits with family were through the large glass picture window of the MQF. Here, Mrs. Armstrong, Aldrin, and Collins visit the Apollo 11 crew.

President Richard M. Nixon welcomes the crew after their historic journey to the Moon.

Mars Pathfinder Lander and Sojourner Rover

Sojourner Begins Its Martian Odyssey
July 1997

Mars Pathfinder was the first spacecraft to land on the red planet since the two Viking landers in 1976. It was launched on December 4, 1996, and reached Mars on July 4, 1997. The spacecraft entered the planet's thin atmosphere, was slowed by a parachute and then rockets, and landed by bouncing on inflated airbags. Its protective aeroshell then unfolded to provide three flat platforms, one of which held the Sojourner rover. Sojourner traveled down a ramp, studied the Martian surface, took images, and examined surface composition with an X-ray spectrometer.

The lander and airbags displayed here are full-scale engineering prototypes. The rover is a full-scale, nonfunctional model built by NASA's Jet Propulsion Laboratory for exhibit at the Museum.

VEHICLE SPECIFICATIONS

Height:	1.5 m (5 ft)
Width:	2.8 m (9 ft 1 in)
Length:	3.2 m (10 ft 6 in)
Weight:	890 kg (1,962 lb) at launch
Manufacturer:	NASA Jet Propulsion Laboratory

MIDDLE
This is the first contiguous, uniform 360-degree color panorama taken by the Imager for Mars Pathfinder (IMP) over the course of sols 8, 9, and 10 (Martian days). Different regions were imaged at different times over the three Martian days to acquire consistent lighting and shadow conditions for all areas of the panorama.

BOTTOM
Engineers test huge, multi-lobed air bags, which will envelope and protect the Mars Pathfinder spacecraft before it impacts the surface of Mars. The bags measure 5 meters (17 feet) tall and about 5 meters (17 feet) in diameter.

Spartan 201 Satellite

This satellite was flown five times on the Space Shuttle from 1993 through 1998. Each time, it was released into space by the Shuttle's remote manipulator arm and retrieved two days later. It houses two instruments, one from the Smithsonian Astrophysical Observatory and one from the Goddard Space Flight Center. Each instrument has a special telescope that creates an artificial solar eclipse in order to observe and determine the nature of the extended solar corona, the Sun's faint outer atmosphere. One instrument spreads ultraviolet light into a spectrum, and the other makes visible light images.

VEHICLE SPECIFICATIONS

Height:	1.5 m (5 ft)
Length:	2.1 m (7 ft)
Width:	3.7 m (12 ft)
Manufacturers:	NASA Goddard Space Flight Center, Smithsonian Astrophysical Observatory, High Altitude Observatory, and Swales Inc.

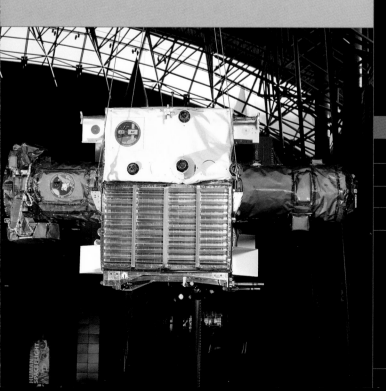

Vega Solar System Probe Bus and Landing Apparatus

In 1984 the Soviet Union launched the Vega 1 and Vega 2 spacecraft, which flew by Venus and dispatched atmospheric instruments and landers, then went on to pass through the tail of Comet Halley. The multinational mission involved scientists and instruments from Bulgaria, Czechoslovakia, France, East and West Germany, Hungary, Poland, the United States, and the Soviet Union, and marked a new era of international cooperation for the Soviet space program.

French scientists designed Vega's main Venus experiment, a balloon carrying scientific instruments that was released into the atmosphere to measure cloud activity. Each Vega also released a Soviet-designed lander to investigate the planet's surface. This bus, for carrying the atmospheric experiment, and the landing apparatus are engineering models.

VEHICLE SPECIFICATIONS

Height:	4.9 m (16 ft 1 in)
Width:	9.2 m (30 ft 3 in)
Weight:	4,000 kg (8,819 lb)
Manufacturer:	Lavochkin Scientific Production Association

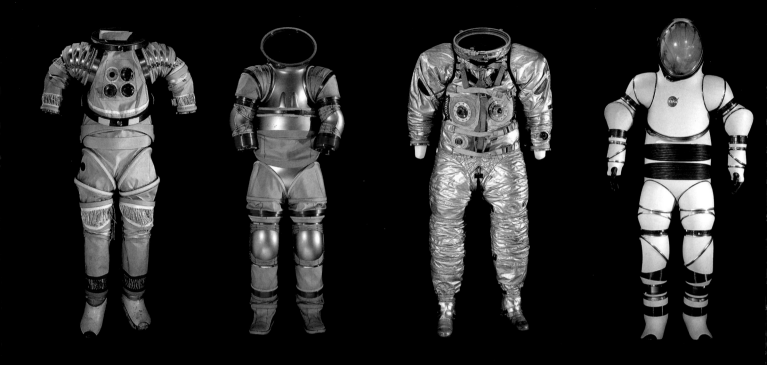

Advanced Spacesuits

TOP LEFT TO RIGHT

B1-A Advanced Extra-Vehicular Pressure suit

Constructed by Litton Industries for NASA—early 1960s

Designed to maintain almost perfect volume while permitting a full range of body motions

AX-3 Advanced Extra-Vehicular Pressure suit

Designed and constructed at NASA—Ames Research Center—mid-1970s

Modular, single-wall laminate suit, designaed to operate at 8 psi—very easy to operate

A4-H Apollo developmental suit

Constructed by ILC Industries for Hamilton Standard—1964

Fourth in series of Apollo developmental suits, with aluminized coating for vacuum chamber thermal testing

AX-2 Advanced Extra-Vehicular Pressure suit

Designed and constructed at NASA—Ames Research

THROUGHOUT THE SPACE PROGRAM, NASA explored several alternatives for full-pressure spacesuits for use outside a spacecraft, including the Advanced Extra-Vehicular Suit (AES). Development of the AES program began in the 1960s, primarily for long-term lunar exploration. The AES is a "hard" suit—it maintains a constant volume when pressurized. This makes it easier to flex the joints, and it eliminates the need for an elaborate internal restraint system to control the "ballooning" effect of pressurization that occurs in "soft" suits. Because it operates at a higher internal pressure than the soft suits used during the Apollo program, the AES requires a less lengthy oxygen pre-breathe period to reduce the risk of an astronaut getting the "bends."

The suit materials were designed to protect against micrometeoroids, and the constant volume and advanced joints made it easier for an astronaut to perform tasks while wearing the suit. The suits were relatively comfortable—an internal harness supported their weight, and they could be individually sized. However, they were never used on a mission, in part because NASA abandoned plans for extended lunar exploration. The advanced suit research undertaken by NASA Ames Research Center has found its way into underwater exploration, and Mars suit research continues to build on the suits developed for the first lunar exploration.

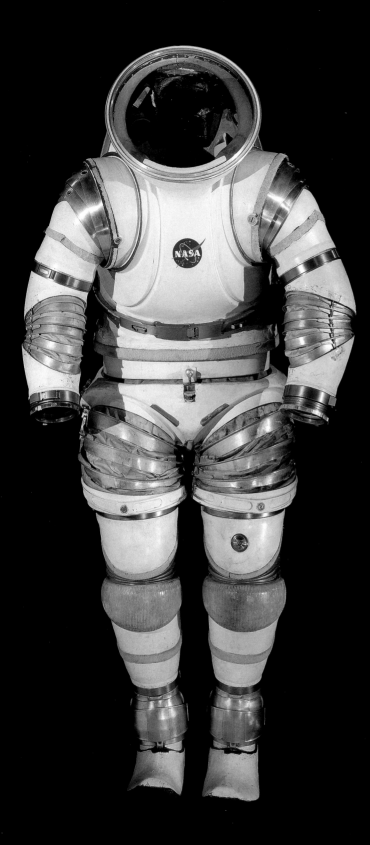

RX-2-A Advanced Extra-Vehicular Pressure suit

Constructed by Litton Industries for NASA—early 1960s

More sophisticated rolling convolute joints with dual-plane closure, operated at 5 psi

Doll in Mercury-style spacesuit—c. 1962

Constructed by BF Goodrich in early 1960s

Designed to be given to VIPs for goodwill and publicity purposes—less than 10 known to have been made

Applications Satellites

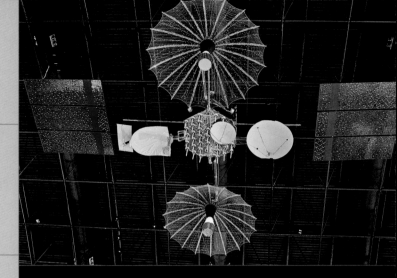

Relay 1 Communications Satellite

Launched by NASA in 1962, Relay 1 was one of several satellites placed in orbit in the decade after Sputnik to test the possibilities of communications from space. Relay 1 received telephone and television signals from Earth and then transmitted them to other locations. The satellite relayed signals between North America and Europe and between North and South America, and it also monitored the effects of radiation on its electronics. In conjunction with the Syncom 3 communications satellite, Relay 1 transmitted television coverage of the 1964 Olympics in Japan.

This prototype of Relay 1 is covered with solar cells and was designed to be spin-stabilized in orbit. The antenna on top is for receiving and transmitting communications signals; those at its base are for telemetry, tracking, and control.

VEHICLE SPECIFICATIONS

Height:	1.3 m (4 ft 4 in)
Width:	0.8 m (2 ft 6 in)
Manufacturer:	RCA

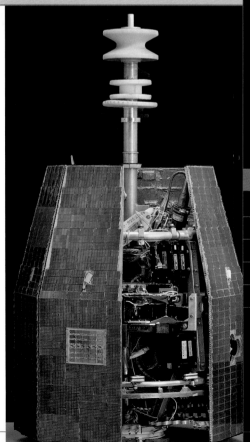

Tracking and Data Relay Satellite

During the first decades of the Space Age, NASA required a worldwide network of ground stations to communicate with satellites and human-operated spacecraft. The Tracking and Data Relay Satellite (TDRS) system, a constellation of three spacecraft placed into geosynchronous orbit beginning in 1983, was designed to replace this expensive, far-flung system. Positioned equidistant in orbit, they provide nearly continuous contact with spacecraft in low Earth orbit—an especially crucial capability for ensuring the safety of Space Shuttle crews. A TDRS transmits both voice and data communications. Under optimum conditions, it can transfer in a second the equivalent of a 20-volume encyclopedia.

This artifact is a high-fidelity model built by Design Models, Inc., under the direction of TRW, which manufactured the first several TDRS spacecraft.

VEHICLE SPECIFICATIONS

Height:	4.3 m (14 ft)
Length:	17.4 m (57 ft)
Width:	13.1 m (43 ft)
Weight:	816.5 kg (1,800 lb)
Manufacturer:	Design Models, Inc.

Agena-B Upper Stage

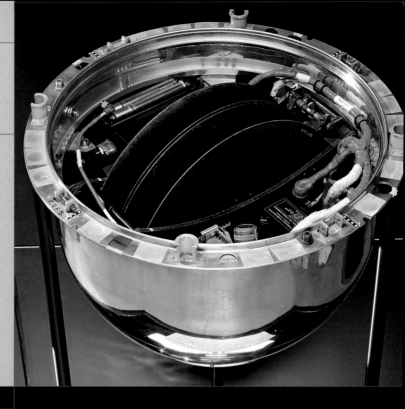

The Agena-B upper stage was used during the 1960s as an orbital injection vehicle for Midas and other satellites and as an intermediate stage booster for Ranger and early Mariner space probes. It was fitted on Thor or Atlas-D launch vehicles, which then became known as Thor-Agena and Atlas-Agena.

Most notably, the Agena-B also served from 1960 to 1963 as the Corona photo-reconnaissance satellite, which flew under the cover name Discoverer. The Agena-B used a restartable and gimballed liquid-fuel rocket engine made by the Bell Aerospace Company. On one side, through the window toward the front, you can see one of the Agena's Earth-sky horizon infrared scanners. This cylindrical optical device kept the vehicle on the right flight path in relation to the horizon.

VEHICLE SPECIFICATIONS

Length:	7.2 m (23 ft 10 in)
Width:	1.5 m (5 ft)
Thrust:	70,400 N (16,000 lb)
Propellants:	nitric acid and UDMH (unsymmetrical dimethyl hydrazine)
Manufacturer:	Lockheed Missiles and Space Co.

Corona Film Return Capsule

Developed by the U.S. Air Force and the Central Intelligence Agency, Corona photoreconnaissance satellites were designed mainly to obtain images of the Soviet Union that manned aircraft could not. The film in a Corona camera was reeled onto a spool in a capsule like this one, which then separated from the satellite and reentered Earth's atmosphere over the Pacific Ocean. The capsule deployed a parachute, which enabled an Air Force airplane to retrieve it by snagging it in midair. General Electric manufactured the capsules.

From 1960 to 1972, more than 120 successful Corona missions provided invaluable intelligence on the Soviet Union and other nations. This capsule was recovered on May 25, 1972, at the end of the last Corona mission. Modern photoreconnaissance satellites return their images electronically.

Human Spaceflight

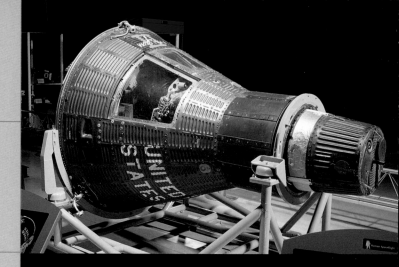

Gemini TTV-1
Paraglider Capsule

At the start of the Gemini program in 1961, NASA considered having the two-astronaut Gemini capsule land on a runway after its return from space, rather than parachute into the ocean. This controlled descent and landing was to be accomplished by deploying an inflatable paraglider wing. However, NASA later decided to stick with the proven technology of parachutes and water landings.

This full-scale, piloted Test Tow Vehicle (TTV) was built to train Gemini astronauts for flight. It served as the first of two TTVs used to perfect maneuvering, control, and landing techniques. A helicopter released the TTV, with its wing deployed, over the dry lake bed at Edwards Air Force Base, California, where it landed.

VEHICLE SPECIFICATIONS

Height:	2.6 m (8 ft 8 in)
Weight:	1,950 kg (4,300 lb)
Manufacturer:	North American Aviation

Mercury Capsule 15B
Freedom 7 II

This Mercury capsule is the only one left showing the complete one-man space-craft in its orbital configuration. It includes the silver and black retrorocket package used to slow the capsule for return to Earth, and the nose section containing the parachutes.

Alan B. Shepard Jr., the first American in space, hoped to fly this Mercury capsule on a long-duration orbital mission in late 1963 called Mercury-Atlas 10 (MA-10). After the success of MA-9, flown by astronaut Gordon Cooper in May 1963, NASA cancelled MA-10 to concentrate on its next human spaceflight project, Gemini. Reflecting Shepard's hope of flying in space again, he had the name *Freedom 7 II* painted on the spacecraft in tribute to his historic 1961 capsule, *Freedom 7.*

VEHICLE SPECIFICATIONS

Length:	2.9 m (9 ft 4 in)
Diameter, heat shield:	1.9 m (6 ft 1 in)
Weight:	1,360 kg (3,000 lb)
Manufacturer:	McDonnell Aircraft Corp.

Gemini VII

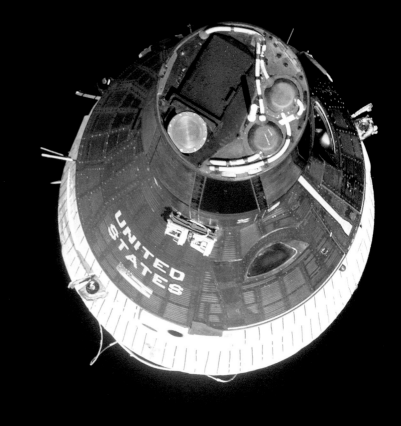

Frank Borman and James A. Lovell Jr. lifted off aboard Gemini VII on December 4, 1965. Their primary mission was to show that humans could live in weightlessness for 14 days, an endurance record that stood until 1970. Their spacecraft also served as the target vehicle for Gemini VI-A, piloted by Walter M. Schirra Jr. and Thomas P. Stafford, who carried out the world's first space rendezvous on December 15. These two achievements were critical steps on the road to the Moon.

The configuration shown here is the only part of Gemini that returned to Earth. Behind the heat shield was an adapter section containing propellants for the maneuvering thrusters, fuel cells for electric power, and retrorockets to return to Earth. It was jettisoned before reentry. The nose section was discarded during deployment of the main parachute, and the spacecraft landed on the ocean with the hatches facing up.

VEHICLE SPECIFICATIONS

Length:	2.7 m (9 ft)
Diameter, heat shield:	2.3 m (7 ft 5 in)
Weight, launch:	3,670 kg (8,074 lb)
Weight, landing:	1,500 kg (3,300 lb)
Manufacturer:	McDonnell Aircraft Corp.

ABOVE RIGHT
This photograph taken on December 15, 1965 shows the Gemini 7 spacecraft as it was observed from the hatch window of the Gemini 6 spacecraft during rendezvous maneuvers and station keeping at a distance of approximately 9 feet apart.

RIGHT
The Gemini VII as an artifact on display

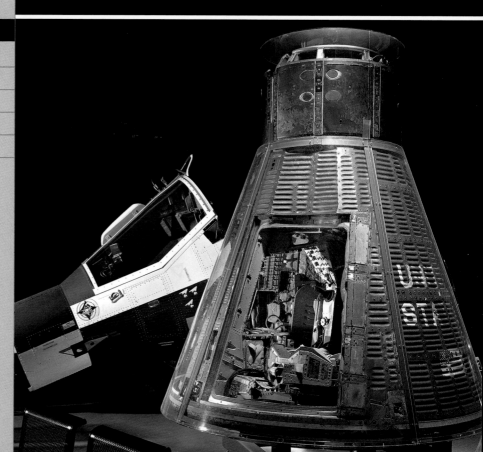

Apollo Boilerplate Command Module

NASA built several "boilerplate" Apollo command modules for testing and to train astronauts and other mission crew members. This one is made of aluminum with a fiberglass outer shell and has an actual command module hatch. It was used by Apollo astronauts, including the crew of Apollo 11, the first lunar landing mission, to practice routine and emergency exits. The interior was later fitted with actual or mockup components to simulate the Apollo-Soyuz spacecraft and the five-person rescue vehicle planned for use if an emergency developed during the Skylab program.

Boilerplate #1102A is displayed here with the flotation collar and bags that were attached to the Apollo 11 command module *Columbia* when it landed in the ocean at the end of its historic mission.

VEHICLE SPECIFICATIONS

Height:	3.2 m (10 ft 7 in)
Weight:	1,814 kg (4,000 lb)
Manufacturer:	North American Aviation

Saturn V Instrument Unit

The Saturn V rocket, which sent astronauts to the Moon, used inertial guidance, a self-contained system that guided the rocket's trajectory. The rocket booster had a guidance system separate from those on the command and lunar modules. It was contained in an instrument unit like this one, a ring located between the rocket's third stage and the command and lunar modules. The ring contained the basic guidance system components—a stable platform, accelerometers, a digital computer, and control electronics—as well as radar, telemetry, and other units.

The instrument unit's stable platform was based on the one used in the German V-2 rocket of World War II. The Bendix Corporation produced the platform, while IBM designed and built the unit's digital computer.

OPPOSITE PAGE
A technician works atop the white room through which the Apollo astronauts will enter their spacecraft, which is stacked at the top of a Saturn V rocket. The vehicle is being prepared for the first manned lunar landing mission. The capsule is easy enough to locate atop the Saturn V rocket, while the location of the instrument unit on the rocket is marked by the telltale black ring at the top of the third stage.

German World War II Aircraft

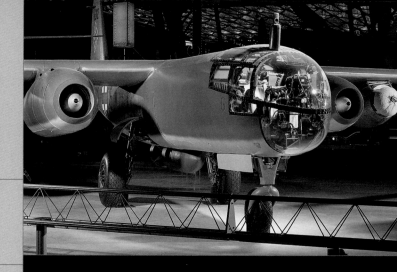

Heinkel He 219 A Uhu

Heavily armed with up to eight cannons and guided to its target by radar, the Heinkel He 219 Uhu (Eagle Owl) was one of the Luftwaffe's most formidable night fighters. It was the first German aircraft fitted with a steerable nosewheel, and the first aircraft in history to enter service fitted with ejection seats. On the aircraft's first mission in 1943, a single He 219 shot down at least five British bombers.

The Museum's airplane is an He 219 A-2 built in late 1944 and the sole survivor of its type. Little is known about its wartime operational history. British forces captured the airplane at Grove, Denmark, in May 1945 and turned it over to the U.S. Army Air Forces for evaluation and testing. Shipped to Freeman Field, Indiana, it was flown for less than 13 hours before being transferred to the Smithsonian.

AIRCRAFT SPECIFICATIONS

Wingspan:	18.5 m (60 ft 8 in)
Length:	15.3 m (50 ft 2 in)
Height:	4.1 m (13 ft 5 in)
Weight, empty:	11,200 kg (24,700 lb)
Top speed:	611 km/h (382 mph)
Engines:	2 Daimler Benz DB 603A, 12-cylinder, liquid-cooled, 1,750 hp
Crew:	2
Armament:	Two MK 108 30 mm cannons, four MG 151/20 20 mm cannons
Manufacturer:	Ernst Heinkel Flugzeugwerke AG, Vienna-Schwechat, Austria, 1944

Arado Ar 234 B Blitz

The Arado Ar 234 B Blitz (Lightning) was the world's first operational jet bomber and reconnaissance aircraft. The first Ar 234 combat mission, a reconnaissance flight over the Allied beachhead in Normandy, took place August 2, 1944. With a maximum speed of 735 kilometers (459 miles) per hour, the Blitz easily eluded Allied piston-engine fighters. While less famous than the Messerschmitt Me 262 jet fighters, the Ar 234s that reached Luftwaffe units provided excellent service, especially as reconnaissance aircraft.

This Ar 234 B-2 served with bomber unit KG 76 from December 1944 until May 1945, when British forces captured it in Norway. Turned over to the United States, it was brought to Wright Field, Ohio, in 1946 for flight testing. In 1949 it was transferred to the Smithsonian, which restored it in 1984–89. This Arado is the sole survivor of its type.

AIRCRAFT SPECIFICATIONS

Wingspan:	14.4 m (47 ft 4 in)
Length:	12.6 m (41 ft 6 in)
Height:	4.3 m (14 ft 2 in)
Weight, empty:	4,900 kg (10,800 lb)
Weight, gross:	10,010 kg (22,070 lb) with RATO (rocket-assisted takeoff) units
Top speed:	735 km/h (459 mph)
Engines:	2 Junkers Jumo 004 B-1 turbojets, 900 kg (1,980 lb) thrust; 2 Walter RATO units, 500-kg (1,100-lb) thrust
Ordnance:	one 1,000-kg or two 500-kg bombs
Manufacturer:	Arado Flugzeugwerke, Alt Lönnewitz, Germany, 1944

Focke-Wulf Fw 190 F

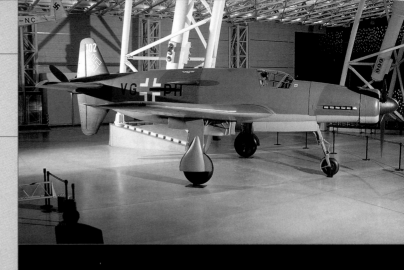

Nicknamed the Würger (Butcher Bird), the Fw 190 entered service in 1941 and flew throughout World War II on all fronts. It was the only German single-seat fighter powered by a radial engine and the only fighter of the war with electrically operated landing gear and flaps. Some served as fighter-bombers with ground attack units, but the Fw 190 is best known for defending against Allied daylight bombing attacks.

This Fw 190 F-8 was originally manufactured as an Fw 190 A-7 fighter. During 1944 it was remanufactured as a fighter-bomber and issued to ground attack unit SG 2. After Germany's surrender it was shipped to Freeman Field, Indiana, then transferred to the Smithsonian in 1949. Its 1980–83 restoration revealed a succession of color schemes. It now appears as it did while serving with SG 2 in 1944.

AIRCRAFT SPECIFICATIONS

Wingspan:	10.5 m (34 ft 6 in)
Length:	9 m (29 ft 6 in)
Height:	4 m (13 ft)
Weight, empty:	3,060 kg (6,750 lb)
Weight, gross:	4,865 kg (10,725 lb)
Top speed:	644 km/h (400 mph)
Engine:	BMW 801 D-2, 14-cylinder, air-cooled, twin-row radial, 1,730 hp
Armament:	two MG 131 13 mm machine guns, two MG 151/20 20 mm cannons
Ordnance:	one 250-kg and four 50-kg bombs
Manufacturer:	Arado Flugzeugwerke, Warnemünde, Germany, 1943

Donier Do 335 A Pfeil

The unique Dornier Do 335 Pfeil (Arrow) was among the fastest piston-engine aircraft ever built. The unconventional push-pull arrangement of its fore and aft propellers provided the power of two engines but with less drag and better maneuverability. The Do 335 first flew in September 1943. Fighter, trainer, reconnaissance, and night fighter versions were planned, but the war ended before large-scale production could begin.

This airplane, a Do 335 A-0, is one of 10 preproduction aircraft and the sole survivor of its type. U.S. Army forces captured it at the Dornier factory at Rechlin-Oberpfaffenhofen on April 22, 1945. The U.S. Navy flight tested it at the Patuxent River Naval Air Station from 1945 to 1948. The Smithsonian acquired it in 1961. In 1974 it was returned to Germany, restored by Dornier, and displayed at the Deutsches Museum in Munich until 1991.

AIRCRAFT SPECIFICATIONS

Wingspan:	13.8 m (45 ft 3 in)
Length:	13.9 m (45 ft 5 in)
Height:	5 m (16 ft 5 in)
Weight, empty:	7,400 kg (16,314 lb)
Top speed:	763 km/h (474 mph)
Engines:	2 Daimler Benz DB 603A, 12-cylinder, liquid-cooled, 1,750 hp
Crew:	1
Armament:	MK 103 30 mm cannon, two MG 151/20 20 mm cannons
Manufacturer:	Dornier-Werke GmbH, Rechlin-Oberpfaffenhofen, Germany, 1944

Northrop P-61C
Black Widow

The P-61 Black Widow was the first U.S. aircraft designed to locate and destroy enemy aircraft at night and in bad weather, a feat made possible by on-board radar. The prototype first flew in 1942. P-61 combat operations began just after D-Day, June 6, 1944, when Black Widows flew deep into German airspace, bombing and strafing trains and road traffic. By the end of World War II, Black Widows had seen combat in every theater and had destroyed 127 enemy aircraft and 18 German V-1 buzz bombs.

The Museum's ERF-61C-1-NO Black Widow was delivered to the Army Air Forces in July 1945. It flew in cold-weather tests and, with its guns removed, in the National Thunderstorm Project. The Smithsonian lent it to the National Advisory Committee for Aeronautics (NACA) in 1951–54 to perform drop tests. It ended its career as an Air Force aircraft and all three service paint schemes have been carefully preserved on the tail booms.

AIRCRAFT SPECIFICATIONS

Wingspan:	20 m (66 ft)
Length:	15 m (49 ft 7 in)
Height:	4.5 m (14 ft 8 in)
Weight, empty:	10,637 kg (23,450 lb)
Weight, gross:	16,420 kg (36,200 lb)
Top speed:	684 km/h (425 mph)
Engines	2 Pratt and Whitney R-2800-73 Double Wasp, air-cooled radial, 2,000 hp with turbo supercharger
Crew:	3 (pilot, radar operator, gunner)
Armament:	four 20 mm cannons, four .50 cal machine guns (original configuration)
Manufacturer:	Northrop Aircraft, 1943

Northrop N-1M Flying Wing

John K. "Jack" Northrop's dream of a flying wing became a reality on July 3, 1940, when his N-1M (Northrop Model 1 Mockup) first flew. One of the world's preeminent aircraft designers and creator of the Lockheed Vega and Northrop Alpha, Northrop had experimented with flying wings for over a decade, believing they would have less drag and greater efficiency than conventional designs. His 1929 flying wing, while successful, had twin tail booms and a conventional tail. In the N-1M he created a true flying wing.

Built of plywood around a tubular steel frame, the N-1M was powered by two 65-horsepower Lycoming engines, later replaced with two 120-horsepower Franklins. While its flying characteristics were marginal, the N-1M led to other designs, including the Northrop XB-35 and YB-49 strategic bombers and ultimately the B-2 stealth bomber.

AIRCRAFT SPECIFICATIONS

Wingspan:	11.6 m (38 ft)
Length:	5.2 m (17 ft)
Height:	1.5 m (5 ft)
Weight, gross:	1,814 kg (4,000 lb)
Top speed:	322 km/h (200 mph)
Engine:	2 Franklin 6AC264F2, 120 hp
Manufacturer:	Northrop Aircraft Inc., Hawthorne, Calif., 1940

North American
P-51C Mustang
Excalibur III

On May 29, 1951, Capt. Charles F. Blair flew Excalibur III from Norway across the North Pole to Alaska in a record-setting 10½ hours. Using a system of carefully plotted "sun lines" he developed, Blair was able to navigate with precision where conventional magnetic compasses often failed. Four months earlier, he had flown Excalibur III from New York to London in less than 8 hours, breaking the existing mark by over an hour.

Excalibur III first belonged to famed aviator A. Paul Mantz, who added extra fuel tanks for long-distance racing to this standard P-51C fighter. With it Mantz won the 1946 and 1947 Bendix air race and set a transcontinental speed record in 1947 when the airplane was named Blaze of Noon. Blair purchased it from Mantz in 1949 and renamed it Excalibur III, after the Sikorsky VS-44 flying boat he flew for American Export Airlines.

AIRCRAFT SPECIFICATIONS

Wingspan:	11.3 m (37 ft)
Length:	9.8 m (32 ft 3 in)
Height:	3.9 m (12 ft 10 in)
Weight, empty:	4,445 kg (9,800 lb)
Weight, gross:	5,052 kg (11,800 lb)
Top speed:	700 km/h (435 mph)
Engine:	Packard Merlin V-1650-9, 1,695 hp
Manufacturer:	North American Aviation, Englewood, Calif., 1944

Grumman F8F-2 Bearcat Conquest 1

In 1969 Darryl Greenamyer broke the 30-year-old speed record for piston-engine aircraft held by the German Messerschmitt Me 209 when he reached 777 kilometers (483 miles) per hour in this heavily modified Grumman Bearcat. Greenamyer also won the National Air Races six times with this airplane before he donated it to the Smithsonian in 1977.

Grumman designed the Bearcat late in World War II as a replacement for the F6F Hellcat Navy fighter. It was noted for its exceptional climbing ability and maneuverability. Conquest 1 featured a shorter wingspan than the production Bearcat, a special small bubble canopy, a larger propeller taken from a Douglas A-1 Skyraider, and a propeller spinner from a North American P-51D Mustang. Special high-octane gasoline, fuel additives, and putty-sealed gaps to reduce drag greatly increased its speed.

AIRCRAFT SPECIFICATIONS

Wingspan:	8.7 m (28 ft 6 in)
Length:	8.4 m (27 ft 8 in)
Height:	4.2 m (13 ft 8 in)
Weight, empty:	3,488 kg (7,690 lb)
Weight, gross:	6,121 kg (13,494 lb)
Top speed:	777 km/h (483 mph)
Engine:	Pratt & Whitney R-2800, 3,100 hp (modified)
Manufacturer:	Grumman Aircraft Engineering Corp., Bethpage, New York, 1948

Lockheed Vega Winnie Mae

Flying this specially modified Lockheed 5C Vega, famed aviator Wiley Post set many records and pioneered several aviation technologies. In 1931 Post and navigator Harold Gatty flew it around the world in eight days, and in 1933 Post became the first to fly around the world solo, taking only seven days. In 1935, while wearing the world's first pressure suit, which he helped design, Post flew the Vega into the stratosphere, reaching 547 kilometers (340 miles) per hour while cruising in the jet stream. The Winnie Mae was named for the daughter of F. C. Hall, the original owner and a close friend of Post.

Designed by John K. "Jack" Northrop, the Lockheed Vega first flew in 1927. It was the first aircraft with the NACA cowl, which streamlined the airflow around and through the engine. This decreased drag and increased power plant cooling.

AIRCRAFT SPECIFICATIONS

Wingspan:	12.5 m (41 ft)
Length:	8.4 m (27 ft 6 in)
Height:	2.5 m (8 ft 2 in)
Weight, empty:	1,177 kg (2,595 lb)
Weight, gross:	2,041 kg (4,500 lb)
Top speed:	298 km/h (185 mph)
Engine:	Pratt & Whitney Wasp C, 500 hp
Manufacturer:	Lockheed Aircraft Co., Burbank, Calif., 1931

World War II Naval Aircraft

Vought-Sikorsky OS2U-3 Kingfisher

The Kingfisher was the U.S. Navy's primary ship-based scout and observation aircraft during World War II. Revolutionary spot welding techniques gave it a smooth, nonbuckling fuselage structure. Deflector plate flaps that hung from the wing's trailing edge and spoiler-augmented ailerons functioned like extra flaps to allow slower landing speeds. Most OS2Us operated in the Pacific, where they rescued many downed airmen, including World War I ace Eddie Rickenbacker and the crew of his B 17 Flying Fortress.

In March 1942 this airplane was assigned to the battleship USS *Indiana*. It later underwent a six-month overhaul in California, returned to Pearl Harbor, and rejoined the *Indiana* in March 1944. Lt. j.g. Rollin M. Batten Jr. was awarded the Navy Cross for making a daring rescue in this airplane under heavy enemy fire on July 4, 1944.

AIRCRAFT SPECIFICATIONS

Wingspan:	11 m (35 ft 11 in)
Length:	10.3 m (33 ft 10 in)
Height:	4.6 m (15 ft 2 in)
Weight, empty:	1,870 kg (4,123 lb)
Weight, gross:	2,722 kg (6,000 lb)
Top speed:	275 km/h (171 mph)
Engine:	Pratt & Whitney R-985-AN-8 air-cooled radial, 450 hp
Crew:	2
Armament:	two 7.62 mm machine guns
Ordnance:	295-kg (650-lb) bomb load
Manufacturer:	Vought-Sikorsky Aircraft Div., Stratford, Conn., 1942

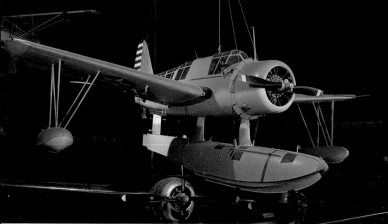

Grumman F6F-3 Hellcat

The Hellcat was originally conceived as an advanced version of the U.S. Navy's F4F Wildcat because development problems had delayed the Wildcat's intended replacement, the Vought F4U Corsair

This F6F-3 Hellcat was delivered to the Navy in 1944 and was assigned to Fighter Squadron 15 (VF-15) on the USS *Hornet*, the first of many assignments. During its three-year operational career, it was damaged in a wheels-up landing, repaired and used for training, and converted to a target drone. Its most notable mission was Operation Crossroads, the atomic bomb tests at Bikini Atoll in 1946. It was launched, unmanned, soon after the first bomb test to obtain data on radioactivity. It was also used to evaluate the first underwater nuclear explosion. Records indicate that its exposure to radioactivity was minimal, and residual radiation is negligible.

AIRCRAFT SPECIFICATIONS

Wingspan:	13 m (42 ft 10 in)
Length:	10.2 m (33 ft 7 in)
Height:	3.4 m (11 ft 1 in)
Weight, empty:	4,092 kg (8,530 lb)
Weight, gross	5,631 kg (12,415 lb)
Engine:	Pratt & Whitney R-2800-10 Double Wasp 18-cylinder, air-cooled radial, 2,000 hp
Armament:	six .50 cal machine guns
Ordnance:	two 500-lb bombs and six rockets
Manufacturer:	Grumman Aircraft Engineering Corp., Bethpage, N.Y., 1944

Vought F4U-1D Corsair

By V-J Day, September 2, 1945, Corsair pilots had amassed an 11:1 kill ratio against enemy aircraft. The aircraft's distinctive inverted gull-wing design allowed ground clearance for the huge, three-bladed Hamilton Standard Hydromatic propeller, which spanned more than 4 meters (13 feet). The Pratt and Whitney R-2800 radial engine and Hydromatic propeller was the largest and one of the most powerful engine-propeller combinations ever flown on a fighter aircraft.

Charles Lindbergh flew bombing missions in a Corsair with Marine Air Group 31 against Japanese strongholds in the Pacific in 1944. This airplane is painted in the colors and markings of the Corsair Sun Setter, a Marine close-support fighter assigned to the USS *Essex* in July 1944.

AIRCRAFT SPECIFICATIONS	
Wingspan:	12.5 m (41 ft)
Length:	10.2 m (33 ft 4 in)
Height:	4.6 m (15 ft), 4.9 m (16 ft 2 in) folded
Weight, empty:	4,037 kg (8,971 lb)
Weight, gross:	6,387 kg (14,080 lb)
Top speed:	671 km/h (417 mph)
Engine:	Pratt & Whitney R-2800-8 air-cooled radial, 2,100 hp
Armament:	six .50 cal M2 machine guns
Ordnance:	eight 5-inch rockets, two 1,000-lb bombs
Manufacturer:	Vought Aircraft Co., Stratford, Conn., 1944

Grumman F-14D(R) Tomcat

This F-14D(R) Tomcat is a deck-launched, supersonic, twin-engine, variable sweep wing, two-place fleet defense and strike fighter. The multiple tasks of navigation, target acquisition, electronic counter measures (ECM), and weapons employment are divided between the pilot and the radar intercept officer (RIO). Primary missions include precision strike against ground targets, air superiority, and fleet air defense.

It is displayed in a configuration that it might have flown near the end of its service life in VF-31 aboard the USS *Abraham Lincoln* while serving in the waters of the Southwest Asian Theater. Two AIM-9 heat-seeking missiles on the outboard pylons, an AIM-7 radar-guided missile on the port pylon, a TARPS pod, an AIM-54 Phoenix missile and Joint Direct Attack Munition (JDAM) are loaded on the belly of the aircraft.

The National Air and Space Museum's Tomcat (BuNo. 159610) was the 157th built during the mid-1970s as an F-14A-85-GR and was one of the few Tomcats that was later modified as an F-14D(R) in the early 1990s. It is credited with one MiG kill which occurred during a fleet defense mission on January 4, 1989, near the coast of Libya.

On January 4, 1989, near the Libyan coast, Two VF-32 F-14As, flying CAP from the USS *John F. Kennedy* (CV-67), were alerted to a pair of Libyan Mikoyan-Gurevich MiG-23 Floggers. The MiG-23s had taken off from Al Bumbaw Airfield near Tobruk. The F-14s locked the MiGs with their powerful AWG-9 radar system. The Tomcats were threatened by the AA-7 Apex missile-carrying Floggers and were cleared to engage the MiGs. During the air battle, the MiGs continued to threaten the Tomcats and finally, after several attempts to evade the MiG radar threat, the incoming pair of MiG-23s was declared hostile and the F-14 crews were cleared to engage them. The crew of the lead F-14A fired an AIM-7 Sparrow missile which did not strike its target, while the second F-14A (BuNo. 159610) found its target destroying one of the MiG-23s with an AIM-7. The lead F-14 re-engaged the remaining MiG-23 firing an AIM-9 Sidewinder heat-seeking missile which detonated in the tailpipe of the Flogger. Both MiG pilots ejected safely from their destroyed aircraft.

AIRCRAFT SPECIFICATIONS

Wingspan unswept:	19.5 m (64 ft 1.5 in)
Wingspan swept:	11.5 m (38 ft 2.5 in)
Length:	18.9 m (62 ft 8 in)
Height:	4.8 m (15 ft 8 in)
Weight, empty:	19,050 kg (42,000 lb)
Weight, gross:	34,019 kg (75,000 lb)
Engine:	Two General Electric F110-GE-400 turbofans (16,090 lb.s.t. dry and 26,795 lb.s.t with afterburning)
Crew:	2; Pilot and Radar Intercept Officer (RIO)
Armament:	Various missiles, bomb packages, and sensor pods
Manufacturer:	Grumman Aircraft Corporation

OPPOSITE TOP
The F-14 was retired from military service in September 2006. Here, the last F-14 makes its final takeoff before landing at the "boneyard" in Tucson, AZ.

OPPOSITE MIDDLE
An F-14D lines up to "catch the wire" aboard an aircraft carrier.

ABOVE
The F-14D(R) was on display at the Udvar-Hazy Center for the "Tomcat Sunset" retirement in September 2006.

BOTTOM
This Tomcat was preserved with the help of F-14 airframe technicians assigned to VF-31 at NAS Oceana.

Mothership Model

Close Encounters of the Third Kind

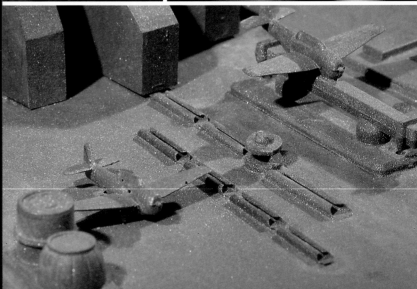

This model of an alien spacecraft was used in the filming of *Close Encounters of the Third Kind,* released by Columbia Pictures in 1977. Director and screenwriter Steven Spielberg envisioned the ship, and a team led by Gregory Jein made it from model train parts and other kits. When filmed with special photographic and lighting effects, the model appeared to be a gigantic craft rising up from behind Devil's Tower in Wyoming. Rotating, colored lights added to the effect.

If you look closely, you can spot some details not seen in the film, including a Volkswagen bus, a submarine, the R2-D2 android from *Star Wars,* a U.S. mailbox, an aircraft, and a small cemetery plot—enhancements added by the model makers as inside jokes.

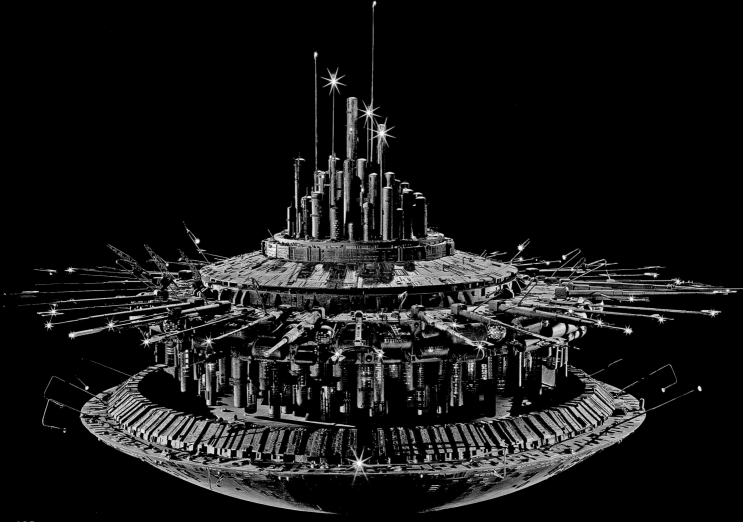

Space Suit Android

This articulated robot was built for NASA's Manned Spacecraft Center in the 1960s for use in spacesuit development. Its hydraulic and electrical actuators replicated many of the human body's joint motions. Sensors throughout the robot measured forces that a suit might exert on a person, so suit designers could determine the force a person would need to exert to move an arm or leg or turn their head. Using this robot enabled testing that might otherwise have been painful, tedious, or even dangerous for a human being.

Photographers' Favorites

THE PHOTOGRAPHERS who document the collections of the National Air and Space Museum are some of the finest artists in the world. To them, an image is not just a picture—it's a story. The stories included on these pages are some of their personal favorites taken at the Steven F. Udvar-Hazy Center.

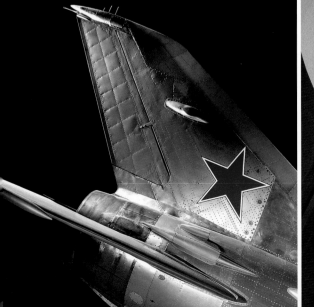

Dane Penland

TOP
SpaceShipOne made a brief stop at the Udvar-Hazy Center so that preparations could be made for its inauguration into the Milestones of Flight Gallery in the Flagship Museum in Washington, DC.

ABOVE
Just after assembly was completed, the Boeing B-29 *Enola Gay* is ready to be elevated into her final display position atop three ten-foot-high electrically driven platforms.

Carolyn Russo

FAR LEFT
Mikoyan-Gurevich MiG-21F-13 "Fishbed C"—Tail Section

LEFT
Hawker Hurricane Mk. IIC—Roundel

Eric Long

LEFT

The Lockheed SR-71 is one of the most beautiful aircraft ever built. In this signature image, it's all about the lighting.

BELOW

The artistic lines of the Udvar-Hazy Center dwarf two members of the construction team as they ascend to the top.

Mark Avino

LEFT

Tenuously extended more than ten stories aloft, this welder secures a joint on the pinnacle of the Center's outside structure. The building was completed ahead of schedule and under budget.

BELOW

An American flag waved from high atop the Udvar-Hazy Center during construction each and every day.

R. Craig Parham

LEFT

Frozen as a reflection in the sculpture called *Ascent* is the Admiral Donald D. Engen Observation Tower. A departing airliner flies overhead, adding a real aviation feel to the Udvar-Hazy Center.

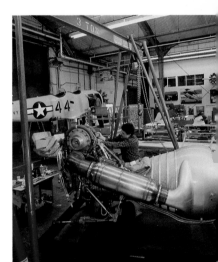

Mr. Paul E. Garber

Restoration

THE PAUL E. GARBER Preservation, Restoration, and Storage Facility is where the rubber meets the road and the hard work of rebuilding and saving the nation's air and space artifact collections takes place. To all of us at NASM, it is simply called "Garber."

The facility is named in honor of Paul Edward Garber (1899–1992), who was instrumental in collecting more than half of the Smithsonian-owned aircraft on display at the facility named in his honor, at the National Air and Space Museum (NASM) on the Mall and, on loan, at other museums around the world. He fell under the spell of both aviation and the Smithsonian while growing up in Washington, D.C. As a 10-year-old, he took a streetcar across the Potomac to watch Orville Wright fly the world's first military airplane at Fort Myer, Virginia.

The Garber Facility is a no-frills assembly of about 30 metal buildings belonging to the National Air and Space Museum and other Smithsonian organizations. About 19 buildings are crammed full of airplanes, spacecraft, and a wide variety of associated parts. One building is devoted to a large restoration shop and 3 buildings are for exhibition production. Each artifact at the Garber Facility has a story behind it. Some are notable for a certain historical role they played or for a particular accomplishment; some represent a technological milestone or stage of aeronautical development; some are the sole surviving example of their type. Often an artifact is worth collecting for a combination of reasons. Soon, the majority of these artifacts will reside in the new Udvar-Hazy Center for all to enjoy for the first time since they were collected decades ago.

Gift Wrapped for America

BY THE TIME THE STEVEN F. UDVAR-HAZY CENTER opened on December 15, 2003, more aircraft were moved, hung, and polished than at any other time since the National Air and Space Museum opened on the National Mall in 1976. Nearly 80 aviation and space artifacts awaited visitors on that day. But the best is yet to come. By the time the Center is filled, more than 300 aircraft and spacecraft, thousands of artifacts and dozens of small exhibits will enrich and inspire visitors from around the world.

After the aircraft and spacecraft had been prepared for the opening events, they were carefully wrapped in protective plastic to minimize cleaning and dusting as the opening approached. As aircraft took their places throughout the museum, the Udvar-Hazy Center resembled a child's bedroom—aircraft tacked gingerly to the ceiling and models placed in carefully selected spaces on dressers and desks. But this place contains real planes and spaceships and they have all been preserved for America and the world to enjoy.

OPPOSITE TOP
The aircraft in the aeronautics hangar are gift wrapped in plastic awaiting the Udvar-Hazy Center opening in December 2003.

OPPOSITE BOTTOM
The Chipmunk as it appeared in flight

RIGHT
The Vought F4U-1D Corsair seems ready to land on a carrier deck.

FAR RIGHT
The Turner RT-14 shown with Roscoe Turner's lion, Gilmore

ABOVE LEFT
The Curtiss P-40E Warhawk (Kittyhawk IA) is hoisted into position.

ABOVE RIGHT
The North American F-86A Sabre, America's most formidable fighter over the skies of Korea, is restored and will inspire all who view it at the Udvar-Hazy Center.

BELOW
The Okha-22 Cherry Blossom, built for war, is the last one that remains in the world.

Opening the Steven

THE FIRST EVENT AT THE STEVEN F. UDVAR HAZY CENTER was a well-deserved "Salute to Military Veterans" which featured music by the U.S. Air Force's WW II–style jazz band, "Airmen of Note," remarks by the Chairman of the Joint Chiefs of Staff, General Richard B. Myers, and attendance by more than 4,000 military aviation veterans of World War II through *Iraqi Freedom.* This event marked the beginning of a week of celebrating American aviation and space flight. The Chancellor of the Smithsonian, the Chief Justice of the United States, William H. Rehnquist, accepted the Udvar-Hazy Center on behalf of the Board of Regents and dedicated the building. Vice President Richard B. Cheney and the Secretary of the Smithsonian Institution, Lawrence M. Small, also participated in the ceremony. The museum opened to the public on Monday the 15th of December.

The opening weeks saw huge crowds and hundreds of thousands of awe-struck visitors. After only 11 weeks of operation, more than one-half million had visited the Udvar-Hazy Center—more than 200,000 of these during the first two weeks alone.

But the Udvar-Hazy Center remains far from complete. On the near horizon lies the construction of a new restoration facility that will permit visitors to watch as skilled Air and Space Museum staff prepares the collection for display. The installation of additional historic artifacts will continue until eighty percent of the national aircraft and spacecraft collection is on public display at the Center.

On December 15, 2003, the Udvar-Hazy Center opened its doors to the public. More than 10,000 visited the center that day. These are a few of the images of the large and enthusiastic crowds.

F. Udvar-Hazy Center

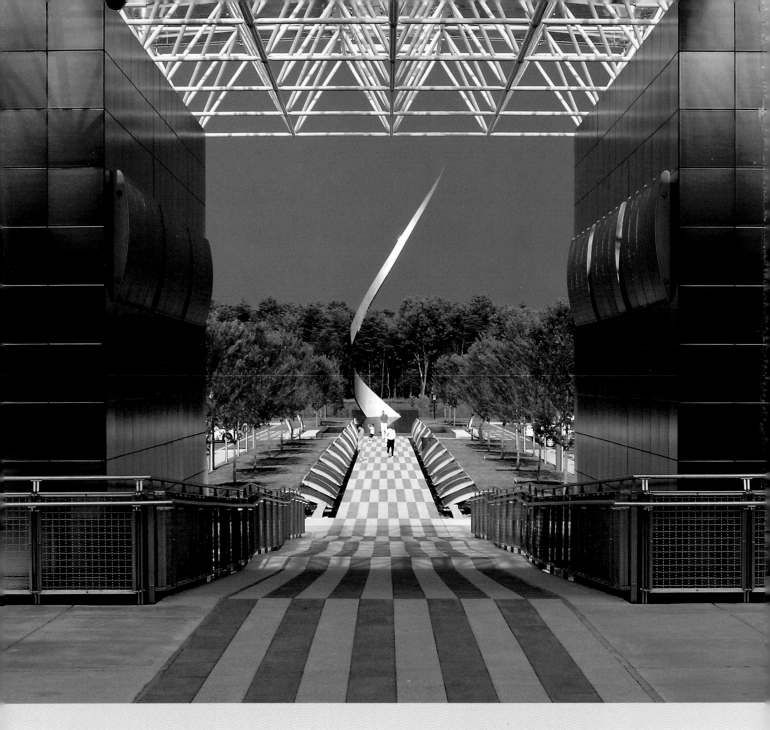

Third Edition 2007
13 12 11 10 09 08 07   10 9 8 7 6 5 4 3 2 1

Library of Congress Control Number: 2007936978

ISBN: 978-09745113-2-0

Front cover: The Museum's Lockheed SR-71A Blackbird

Back cover: Space shuttle (OV-101) *Enterprise*

Inside front and back flaps: Images taken from atop the monstrous hangar doors located at the far ends of the Udvar-Hazy Center looking toward the middle of the building. The Udvar-Hazy Center is more than three football fields long.

This page: Upon exiting the Udvar-Hazy Center, visitors experience a dramatic vista highlighted by John Safer's magical sculpture, *Ascent*.

Photo staff: Mark Avino, Eric Long, Dane Penland, and Carolyn Russo

All images are from the National Air and Space Museum except the following:
Alan D. Toelle (via NASM), page 47
Bell Helicopter Textron (via NASM), page 20
Boeing Company (via NASM), page 34
Jim Qualls, page 65 (graphic image lower right)
National Aeronautics and Space Administration (NASA), pages 40 (top), 52 (center and bottom), 53, (left top and bottom), 78 (all bottom), 79 (all but top left), 80 (top and center), 81 (all), 82 (center and bottom), 89 (top), 90
Shell Companies Foundation, Inc. (via NASM), page 49 (lower right)
Tyson V. Rininger, page 100 (center)
U.S. Navy, page 100 (top)

Edited by Dik A. Daso, Curator of Modern Military Aircraft, National Air and Space Museum
Proofread by Laura Iwasaki and Marie Weiler
Designed by Jeff Wincapaw with assistance by Tina Kim
Color separations by iocolor, Seattle
Produced by Marquand Books, Inc., Seattle
    www.marquand.com
Printed and bound in China by C&C Offset Printing Co., Ltd.